K

TABLE OF CONTENT

PREFACE

The purpose of this guidebook is simple:

To give everyday people, entrepreneurs, business owners, and trustees the same practical understanding of the Uniform Commercial Code (UCC) that banks, corporations, and attorneys use every day.

The UCC can feel complicated when first encountered, not because it is inaccessible, but because most explanations fall into two extremes:

- Overly technical legal commentary
- Misleading fringe interpretations

This guide takes a third path—one that is:

- Clear
- Accurate
- Practical
- State-agnostic
- Based entirely on how the UCC is actually applied

Whether you are managing a trust, establishing a business credit profile, filing for intellectual property security interests, or structuring personal commercial agreements, understanding the UCC is not just useful—it is empowering.

This book avoids myths, jargon, and speculative theories.
Instead, it provides:

- Real filing standards
- True legal definitions
- Practical examples
- Illustrated diagrams
- Step-by-step breakdowns
- Actual Secretary of State practices
- Enforcement-level clarity

It is educational, not legal advice; informative, not ideological.
Every chapter is designed to deepen comprehension and build real skill in filing, maintaining, and enforcing UCC records.

By the end of this book, you will not only understand how UCC filings work—you will understand how secured creditors think, how priority is established, and how private commercial relationships are protected under Article 9.

INTRODUCTION

What This Guide Is — and What It Is Not

What This Guide Is

This guide explains—accurately and without unnecessary complexity—how the UCC filing system actually functions in real commercial practice.

It shows how:

- Secured parties establish priority
- Collateral descriptions must be written
- Trusts and LLCs interact under Article 9
- UCC-1 and UCC-3 filings work together
- Assignments, continuations, and corrections operate
- Multi-state jurisdiction rules apply
- Enforcement and litigation are handled

It distills the core system used by:

- Banks
- Financing companies
- Equipment lenders
- Commercial buyers
- Corporations
- Trust administrators
- Professional secured parties

The UCC is not secret.
It is not mystical.
It is not metaphysical.
It is commercial law—the backbone of the American credit system.

This guide makes that system fully understandable.

What This Guide Is NOT

This book does not:

- Create debt out of thin air
- Alter citizenship or legal status
- Terminate court jurisdiction

INTRODUCTION

- Override statutory law
- Serve as attorney-provided legal advice
- Provide loopholes or fringe remedies

A UCC filing is:

- A public notice
- A declaration of a secured interest
- A documentation of rights between parties

It is *not* a magic wand, exemption, or immunity tool.
It must be supported by real agreements, real value, and real relationships.

This guide is intentionally designed to eliminate confusion caused by misinformation.

Why This Guidebook Matters

Every entrepreneur, creator, property owner, or trustee should understand:

- How rights are secured
- How priority is protected
- How lenders evaluate risk
- How trust-based commercial systems operate
- How to demonstrate authority in financial transactions

People who understand Article 9 hold a dramatic advantage in:

- Business
- Finance
- Asset protection
- Negotiation
- Intellectual property management
- Trust administration

They understand how commercial relationships are structured and protected.

How to Use This Book

You may use this guidebook as:

INTRODUCTION

- A complete educational manual
- A step-by-step filing workbook
- A reference tool for trust or business administration
- A course companion for structured training
- A compliance checklist for filing accuracy
- A resource for negotiation or enforcement preparation

Each chapter builds on the last, creating a progression from foundational knowledge to advanced professional application—including enforcement strategies rarely explained outside legal or banking circles.

The Goal

By the end of this guide, you will be able to:

- Correctly draft a UCC-1
- Perfect a security interest
- Maintain priority over competing creditors
- Understand how to continue, amend, assign, or terminate a filing
- Protect intellectual property and digital assets
- Navigate multi-state jurisdiction rules
- Prepare enforcement-ready documentation
- Build a trust-centered commercial ecosystem

In short:

☞ You will think and operate like a secured party.

Not theoretically—professionally.

Chapter 1
Understanding the UCC Filing System

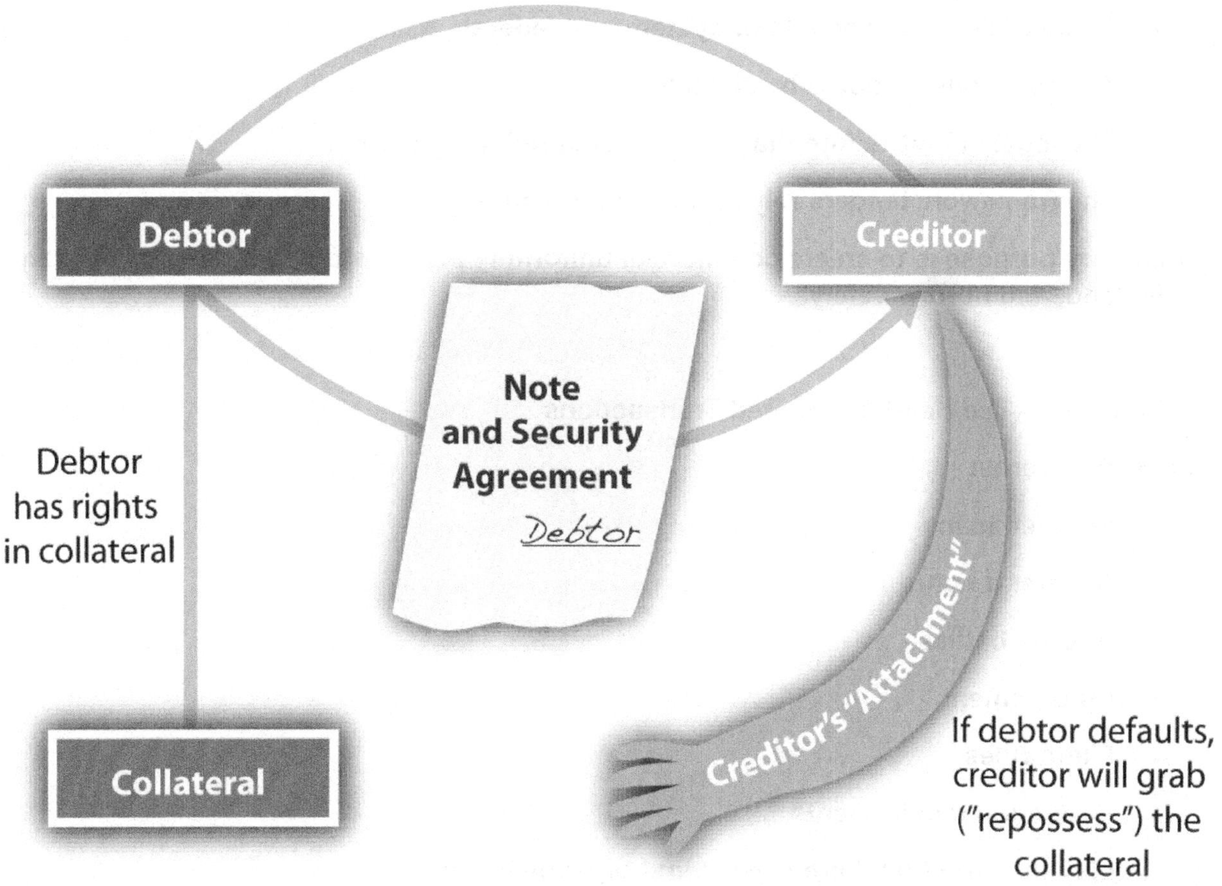

CHAPTER 1 — Understanding the UCC Filing System

Illustrated Edition — Matching the Style of Chapters 2 & 3

I. Introduction to the UCC Framework

The Uniform Commercial Code (UCC) is the backbone of modern American commerce. Every bank, trust, corporation, dealership, and large business relies on it daily.

Despite this, it remains one of the most misunderstood areas of law.

This chapter builds your foundation — everything in later chapters will stack on the concepts introduced here.

"What Is the UCC?"

II. What the Uniform Commercial Code *Is*

Chapter 1
Understanding the UCC Filing System

The UCC is:

- A state-level commercial law system, not federal
- A model code, adopted by all states
- The legal infrastructure that governs secured transactions
- The framework lenders rely on to avoid disputes

Its primary purpose is to create commercial uniformity across states so businesses can trade, lend, and borrow safely.

III. Article 9 — The Heart of Secured Transactions

Article 9 governs:

- Secured loans
- Collateral rights
- Priority battles
- Enforcement
- Filing rules
- Perfection requirements

To simplify the structure, here is your first pipeline image.

IV. The Three Pillars: Attachment → Perfection → Priority (APP)

These three concepts govern *every* secured transaction.

A UCC-1 is only one part of the process.
People misunderstand the UCC because they focus on the filing instead of the legal structure.

To make this unmistakably clear:

The APP Model (Attachment → Perfection → Priority)

A. Attachment

The moment the security interest becomes enforceable between the debtor and secured party.

Requires:

1. Value given
2. Debtor has rights in collateral

3. **Security agreement exists**

B. Perfection

Making the interest enforceable against third parties.

Most commonly achieved by filing a UCC-1.

C. Priority

Determines "who gets paid first" when multiple creditors claim the same collateral.

Rule:

First to file or perfect wins.

V. The UCC Filing System as Public Notice

A UCC filing is not a contract.
It is not proof of a debt.
It is not ownership.
It is not a court order.

It is public notice, nothing more — and nothing less.

To show how the notice system works:

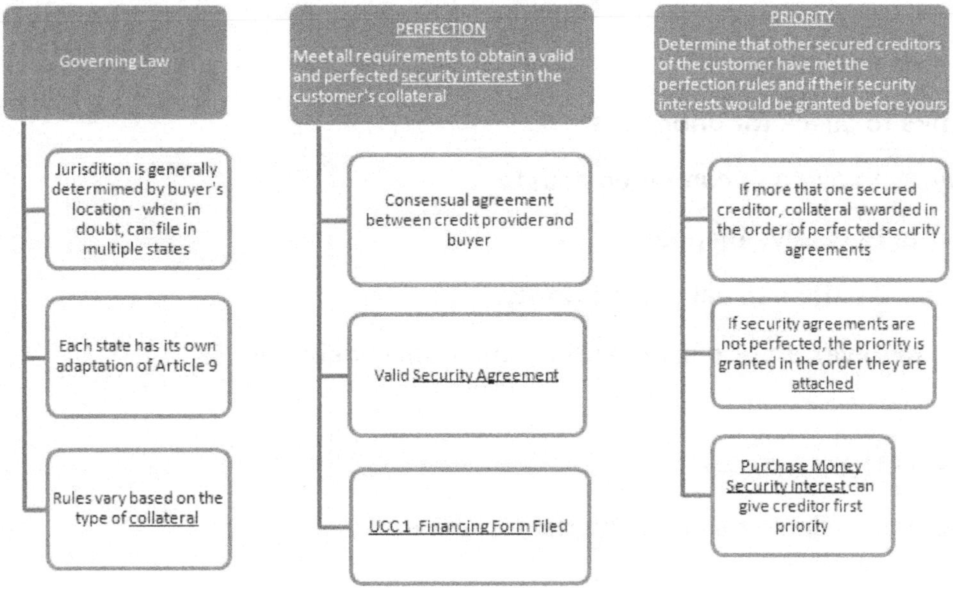

UCC Public Notice Flow (How the Filing Is Used)

Chapter 1
Understanding the UCC Filing System

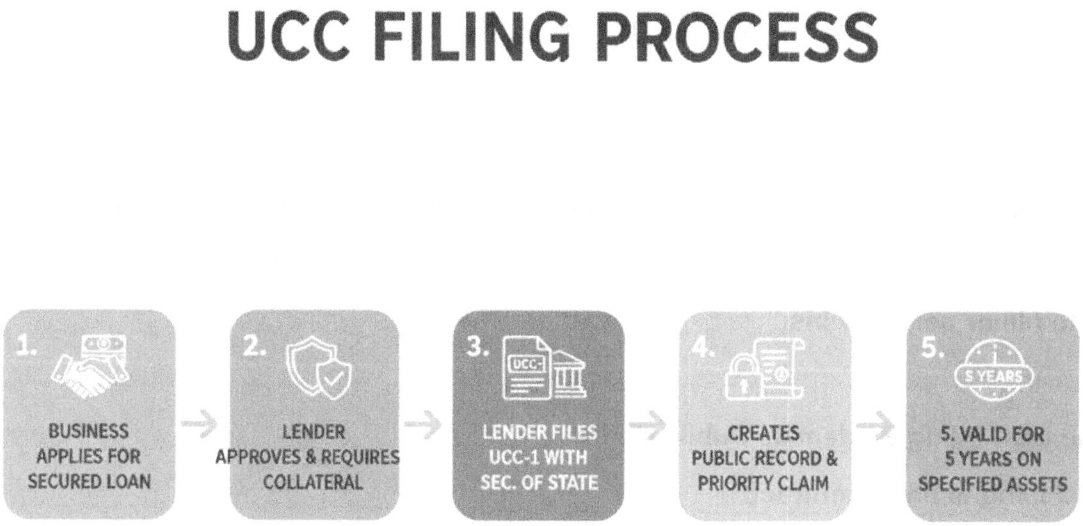

The notice system allows:

- Banks to check for prior liens
- Buyers to avoid encumbered assets
- Courts to resolve disputes
- Secured parties to establish priority

Everything revolves around searchability and public visibility.

VI. Why Exact Names Matter

The UCC database indexes filings by debtor name.
If the name is incorrect:

- The filing becomes "seriously misleading"

- It may be rendered legally ineffective
- Courts may invalidate your priority

Here is a visual to reinforce this rule.

VII. What Happens Behind the Scenes in a Secured Transaction

A secured transaction is not just a filing — it is an entire lifecycle.

Below is your commercial workflow.

The lifecycle includes:

1. Negotiation
2. Security agreement
3. Attachment
4. UCC-1 filing
5. Perfection
6. Priority
7. Amendments
8. Enforcement (if needed)

This lifecycle repeats across trillions of dollars of transactions.

VIII. Misunderstandings and Misuses of the UCC System

Common misconceptions include believing that the UCC:

✗ Creates sovereignty
✗ Cancels debts
✗ Applies to biological persons
✗ Overrides criminal or administrative systems
✗ Is a workaround for court jurisdiction

These ideas do not appear anywhere in Article 9 and are universally rejected by courts.

To clarify correct vs incorrect use cases:

Proper vs Improper Uses of UCC Filings

Chapter 1
Understanding the UCC Filing System

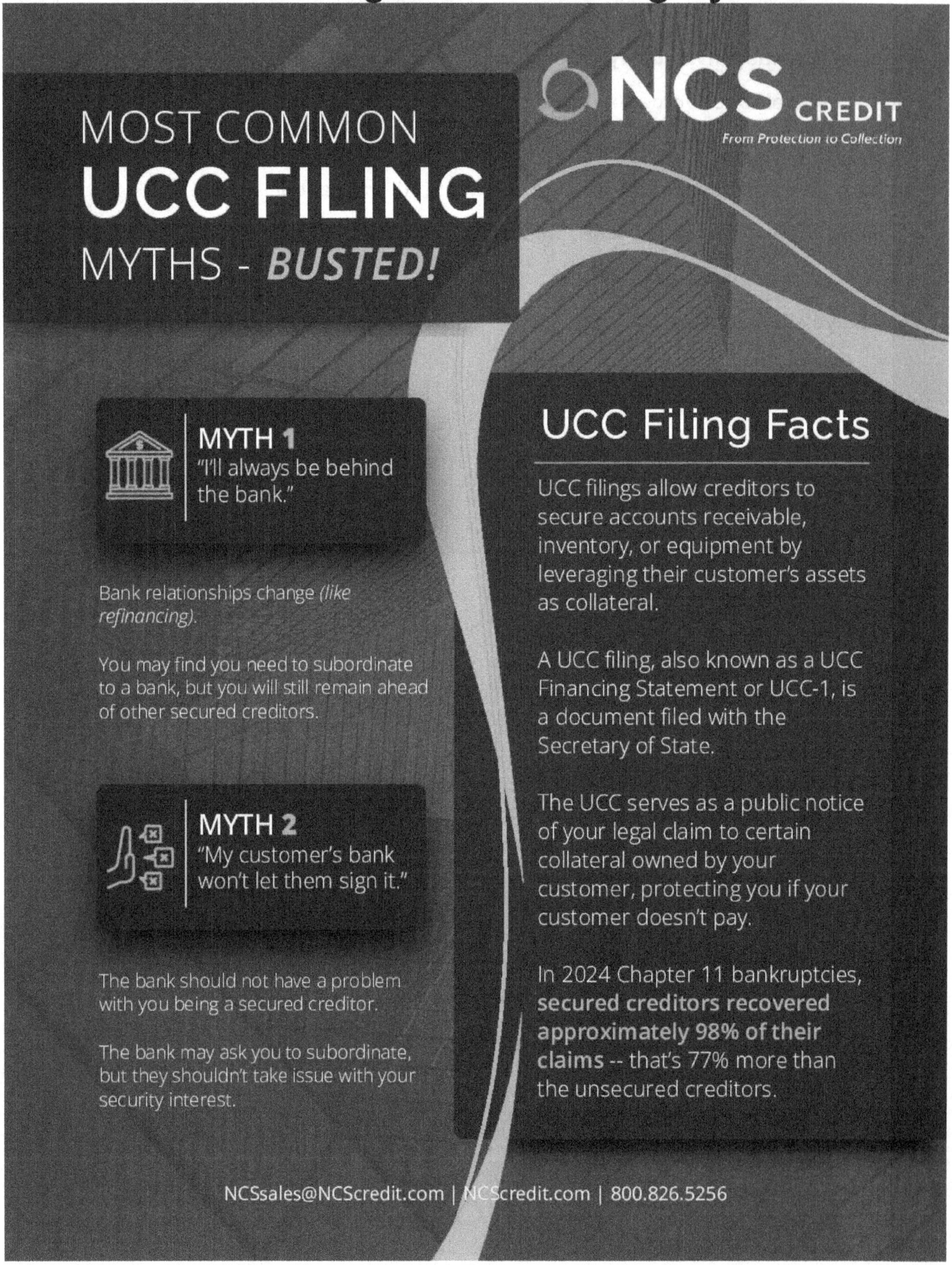

Chapter 1
Understanding the UCC Filing System

UCC FINANCING STATEMENT

FOLLOW INSTRUCTIONS (front and back) CAREFULLY

A. NAME & PHONE OF CONTACT AT FILER [optional]

B. SEND ACKNOWLEDGMENT TO: (Name and Address)

John Henry Smith
c/o 1234 Main Street
Anywhere, uSA [00000]

THE ABOVE SPACE IS FOR FILING OFFICE USE ONLY

1. DEBTOR'S EXACT FULL LEGAL NAME - insert only one debtor name (1a or 1b) - do not abbreviate or combine names

1a. ORGANIZATION'S NAME **SMITH, JOHN H, ORGANIZATION/TRADE NAME/TRADE MARK - DEBTOR**				
OR 1b. INDIVIDUAL'S LAST NAME	FIRST NAME	MIDDLE NAME		SUFFIX
1c. MAILING ADDRESS **C/O BIRTH ADDRESS**	CITY **BIRTH TOWN**	STATE **ST**	POSTAL CODE **11111**	COUNTRY **USA**
1d. TAX ID #: SSN OR EIN **leave blank** | ADD'L INFO RE ORGANIZATION DEBTOR | 1e. TYPE OF ORGANIZATION **ENS LEGIS/TRUST**	1f. JURISDICTION OF ORGANIZATION **Private**	1g. ORGANIZATIONAL ID #, if any **(birth cert # goes here)**		NONE

2. ADDITIONAL DEBTOR'S EXACT FULL LEGAL NAME - insert only one debtor name (2a or 2b) - do not abbreviate or combine names

2a. ORGANIZATION'S NAME **SMITH, SALLY M, ORGANIZATION/TRADE NAME/TRADEMARK - DEBTOR**				
OR 2b. INDIVIDUAL'S LAST NAME	FIRST NAME	MIDDLE NAME		SUFFIX
2c. MAILING ADDRESS **C/O 4321 CENTER STREET**	CITY **BIRTH TOWN**	STATE **ST**	POSTAL CODE **11111**	COUNTRY **USA**
2d. TAX ID #: SSN OR EIN **leave blank** | ADD'L INFO RE ORGANIZATION DEBTOR | 2e. TYPE OF ORGANIZATION **ENS LEGIS/trust**	2f. JURISDICTION OF ORGANIZATION **Private**	2g. ORGANIZATIONAL ID #, if any **(birth cert # goes here)**		NONE

3. SECURED PARTY'S NAME (or NAME of TOTAL ASSIGNEE of ASSIGNOR S/P) - insert only one secured party name (3a or 3b)

3a. ORGANIZATION'S NAME				
OR 3b. INDIVIDUAL'S LAST NAME **Smith**	FIRST NAME **John**	MIDDLE NAME **Henry**		SUFFIX
3c. MAILING ADDRESS **c/o Current Street**	CITY **Resident address**	STATE **state**	POSTAL CODE **[99999]**	COUNTRY **uSA**

4. This FINANCING STATEMENT covers the following collateral:

This is Actual and Constructive Notice that all of Debtor's interest now owned or hereafter acquired is hereby accepted as collateral for securing contractual obligation in favor of the Secured Party as detailed in a true, correct, complete, notarized Security Agreement. Affidavit of Obligation file stamp #______, at the county recorders office on (date of filing) consummated on (Date of the Affidavit of Obligation between debtor and creditor)
NOTICE: In accordance with USC - Property - This is the entry of the Debtor in the Commercial Registry as a transmitting utility and the following property is hereby registered in the same as public notice of a commercial transaction: Certificate of Birth documents #____________; Employer Identification #(SS# w/one dash I.E. 12-3456789); All property is accepted for value and is exempt from Levy. Adjustment of this filing is from Public Policy HJR-192, Public Law 73-10 and UCC 10-104. All proceeds, products, accounts, fixtures and the orders therefrom are released to the Debtor.
SMITH JOHN H, ORGANIZATION/TRADE NAME/TRADE MARK/ TRUST - DEBTOR
SMITH, SALLY M, ORGANIZATION/TRADE NAME/TRADE MARK / TRUST- DEBTOR

5. ALTERNATIVE DESIGNATION [if applicable]: ☐ LESSEE/LESSOR ☐ CONSIGNEE/CONSIGNOR ☐ BAILEE/BAILOR ☐ SELLER/BUYER ☐ AG. LIEN ☐ NON-UCC FILING

6. ☐ This FINANCING STATEMENT is to be filed [for record] (or recorded) in the REAL ESTATE RECORDS. Attach Addendum [if applicable] 7. Check to REQUEST SEARCH REPORT(S) on Debtor(s) [ADDITIONAL FEE] [optional] ☐ All Debtors ☐ Debtor 1 ☐ Debtor 2

8. OPTIONAL FILER REFERENCE DATA

FILING OFFICE COPY — NATIONAL UCC FINANCING STATEMENT (FORM UCC1) (REV. 07/29/98)

Chapter 1
Understanding the UCC Filing System

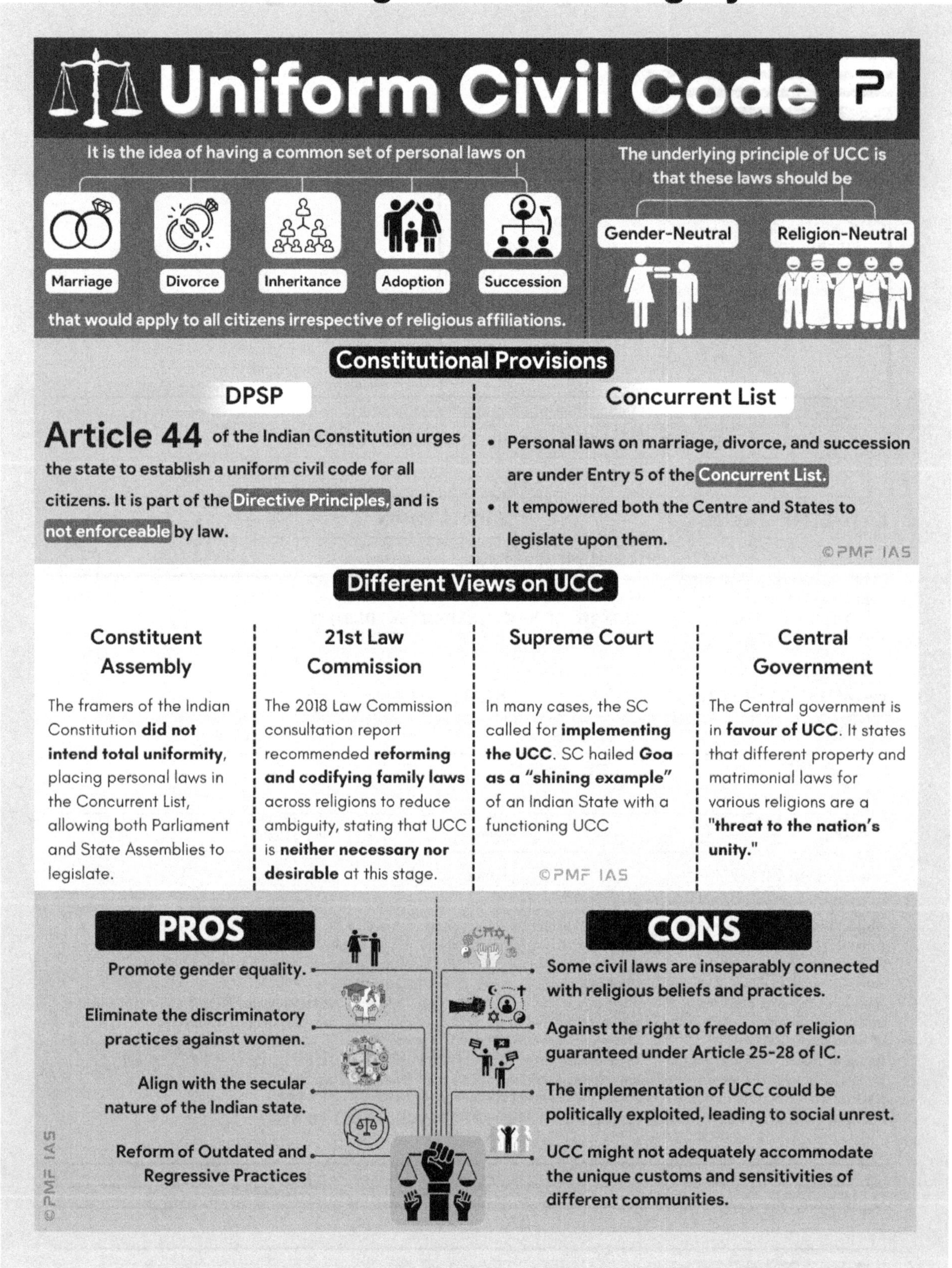

Chapter 1
Understanding the UCC Filing System

IX. Why the Secretary of State Accepts Almost Everything

Filing offices do not:

- Judge validity
- Check contracts
- Investigate claims
- Police misuse

Their role is clerical, not judicial.

They timestamp and index filings.
Courts handle disputes later.

This is why bad filings are accepted —
but not enforceable.

X. A Simple Model for Understanding the Entire UCC System

At its core, the UCC works because of this relationship:

Private Agreement (Substance) → Public Filing (Notice)

To anchor this concept visually:

XI. Why This Chapter Matters Before Moving Forward

Everything in later chapters depends on mastering:

- Attachment
- Perfection
- Priority
- Debtor name precision
- Public notice principles
- Filing hierarchy
- The role of the UCC database

Without this foundation, no one can file effectively — even if they know how to fill out the form.

Chapter 1
Understanding the UCC Filing System

Full Illustrated Edition — Matching the Style of Chapter 3

I. Understanding the Purpose of the UCC-1

A UCC-1 Financing Statement is the core public-notice document used in Article 9 of the Uniform Commercial Code.
It does not create the secured transaction — it simply announces it to the commercial world.

Below is your visual introduction.

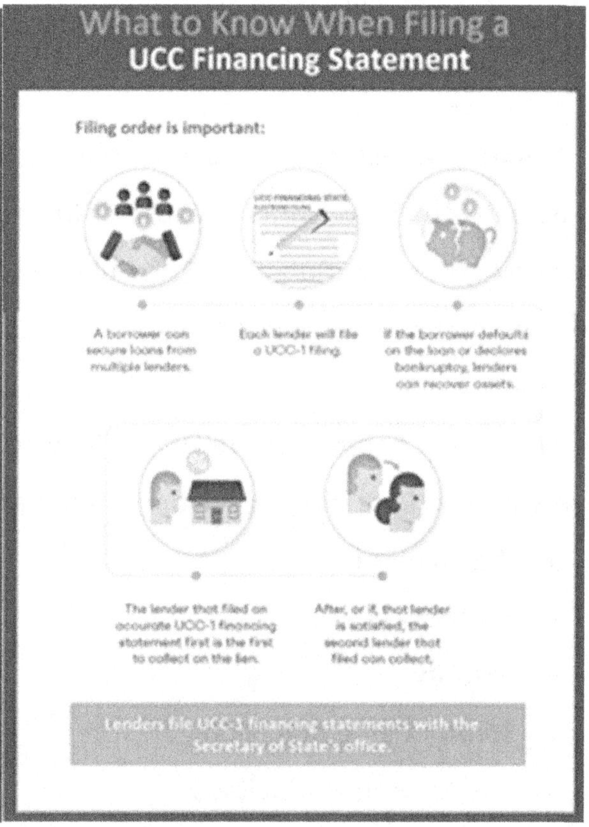

Chapter 1
Understanding the UCC Filing System

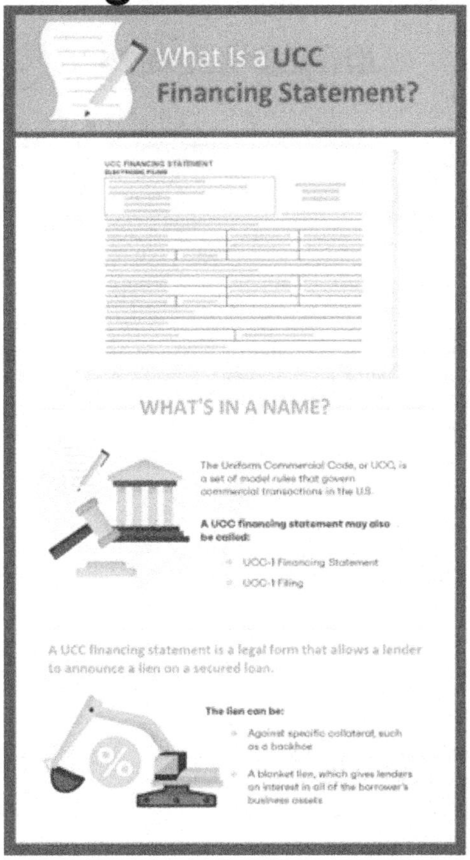

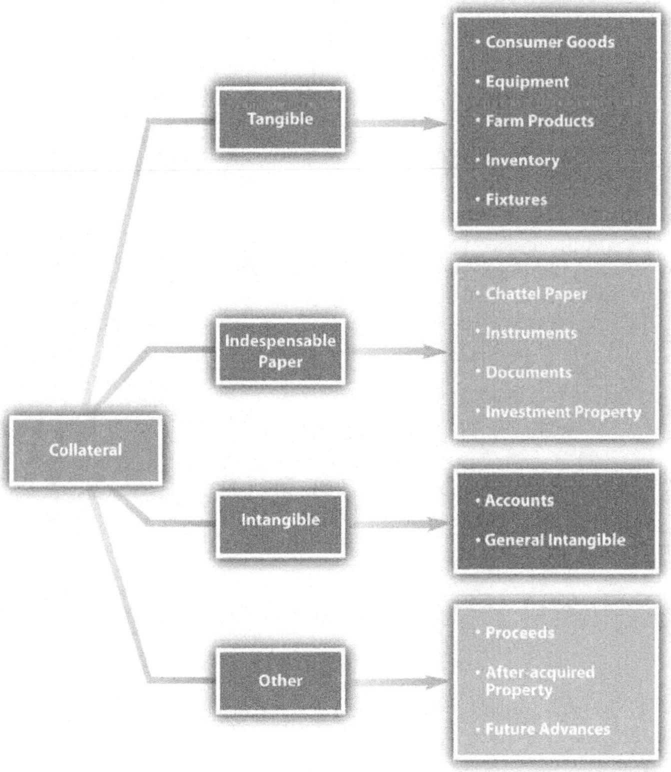

Chapter 1
Understanding the UCC Filing System

UCC 2-207 Analysis

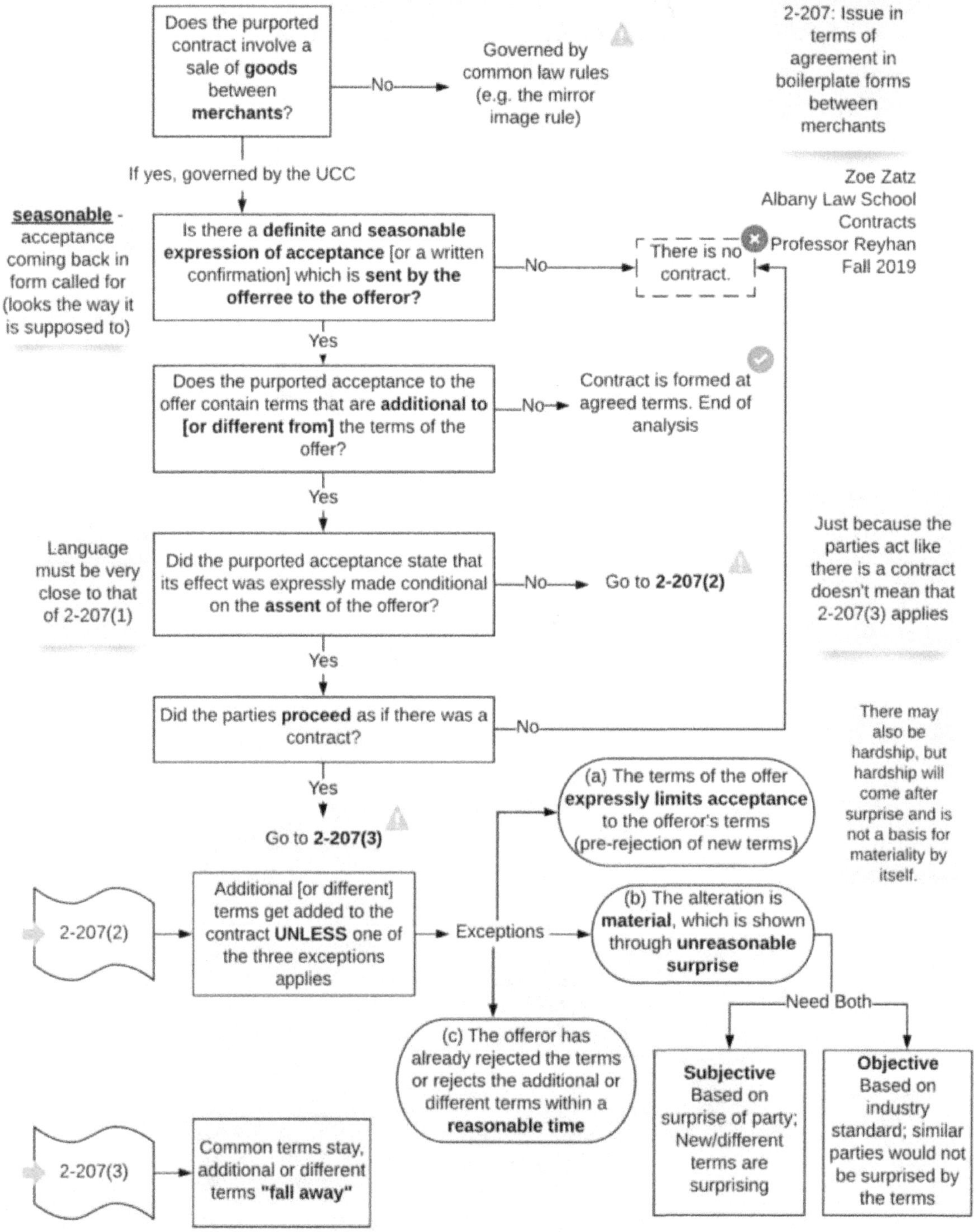

CHAPTER 2

What a UCC-1 Financing Statement Is

II. What the UCC-1 Can and Cannot Do

A major misconception is believing the UCC-1 creates power beyond its scope.
It does not.

Here is a clear, comparison.

✓ A UCC-1 can:

- Establish public notice
- Preserve priority
- Support enforcement *if* the agreement exists
- Timestamp the security interest

✗ A UCC-1 cannot:

- Replace a security agreement
- Transfer ownership
- Prove a debt
- Bind agencies or courts
- Create money or cancel obligations

The difference between notice and substance is the foundation of Article 9.

III. The Anatomy of a UCC-1 Financing Statement

A UCC-1 is structurally simple but legally powerful.

It contains three essential parts:

1. Debtor information
2. Secured party information
3. Collateral description

Here is the visual breakdown.

Image: Anatomy of the UCC-1 Form

Key takeaways:

- The debtor's name must be exact

CHAPTER 2

What a UCC-1 Financing Statement Is

- The secured party must be clearly identified
- The collateral box is the most litigated area
- Optional fields do not affect legal effectiveness

Everything hinges on correctness and clarity.

IV. Collateral Descriptions — Good, Risky, and Invalid

Article 9 allows broad flexibility, but courts require clarity and commercial reasonableness.

Below is a visual explanation of acceptable vs. unacceptable descriptions.

Image: Good vs. Bad Collateral Descriptions

✓ Valid Example

"All equipment, inventory, accounts, general intangibles, and proceeds."

⚠ Borderline Example

"All assets of the debtor."
(Allowed, but only if the security agreement supports it.)

✗ Invalid Example

"The living man, body, soul, DNA, and all derivatives thereof."
(Not recognized as collateral under Article 9.)

Your guidebook avoids every pitfall that leads to ineffective filings.

V. The UCC Filing Hierarchy — Why the Contract Still Controls

A UCC-1 does not create rights; it announces them.

The real legal structure looks like this.

Image: Filing Hierarchy — Security Agreement → UCC-1 → Amendments

Breakdown:

- Security Agreement — creates enforceable rights
- UCC-1 Filing — perfects the interest via public notice

CHAPTER 2

What a UCC-1 Financing Statement Is

- UCC-3 Amendments — continue, modify, assign, or terminate

The UCC-1 is therefore not the transaction, but a public record of it.

VI. When a UCC-1 Is Filed — Timing and Strategy

A secured party may file:

- Before attachment ("early filing" — fully allowed)
- During the transaction
- After attachment

Priority depends almost entirely on the timestamp.

To embed this visually into the reader's memory:

This lifecycle is the core of UCC practice nationwide.

CHAPTER 2

What a UCC-1 Financing Statement Is

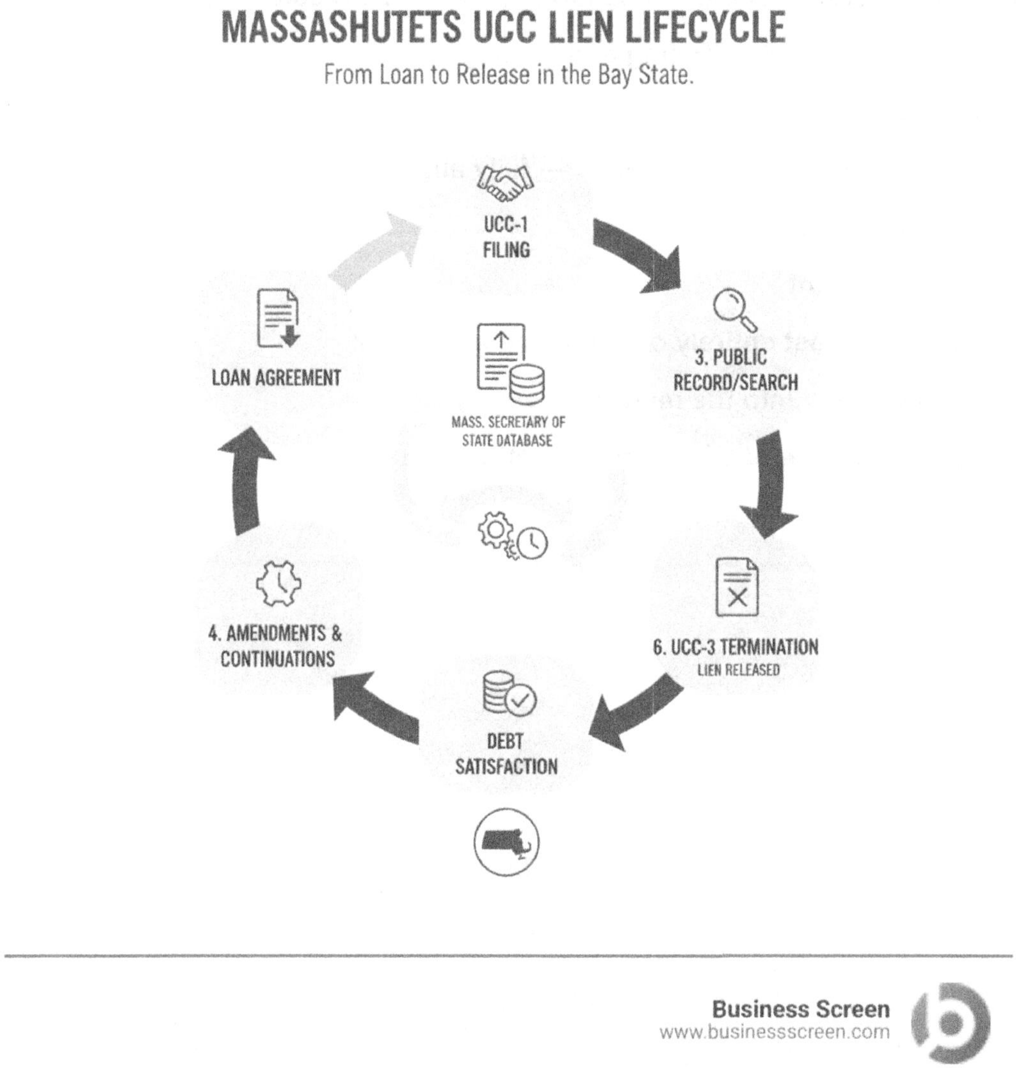

VII. Debtor Name Accuracy — The Most Critical Requirement

99% of ineffective filings fail because the debtor name was:

- **Misspelled**
- **Shortened**
- **Missing suffixes (LLC, Inc.)**
- **Pulled from a DBA instead of legal entity name**

CHAPTER 2

What a UCC-1 Financing Statement Is

Correct patterns:

- **Individuals → Name on government ID**
- **LLCs → Exact name including "LLC"**
- **Corporations → Exact name including "Inc."**
- **Trusts → Trust name, not trustee name**
- **Estates → "Estate of [Name], deceased"**

Incorrect patterns:

- **DBAs (not valid debtor names)**
- **Nicknames**
- **Missing suffixes or punctuation**

A single character can destroy perfection.

VIII. The UCC Public Notice System — How Your Filing Is Used

Once filed, your UCC-1 becomes part of a national commercial ecosystem.

Lenders, buyers, and courts rely on your filing to determine:

- **Risk**
- **Ownership encumbrances**
- **Priority**
- **Validity of transfers**

Here's the illustrated map.

UCC Public Notice Ecosystem

CHAPTER 2

What a UCC-1 Financing Statement Is

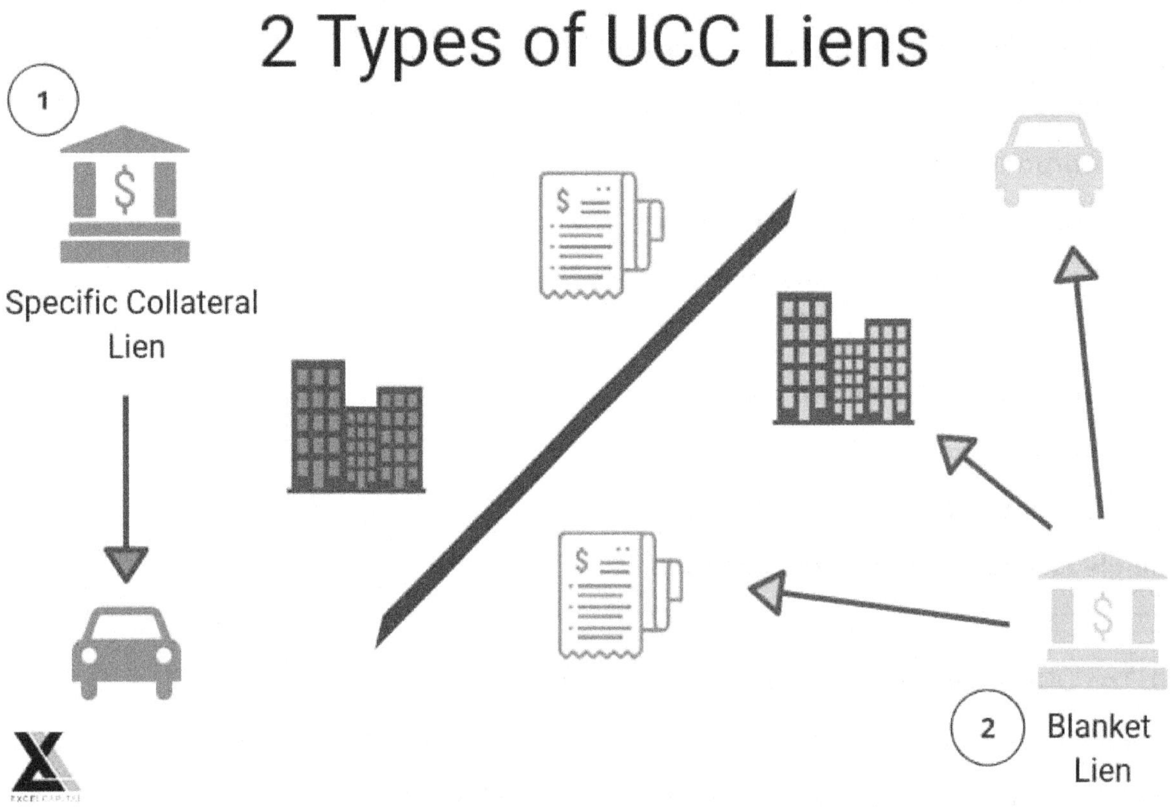

This visual demonstrates:

- **How lenders check for prior filings**
- **How buyers determine whether assets are encumbered**
- **How courts verify priority in disputes**

Your filing must be searchable and precise — or it is invisible.

IX. Why UCC-1 Filings Do Not Require Signatures

Because:

- **The security agreement contains the signatures**
- **The UCC-1 is only notice**

CHAPTER 2

What a UCC-1 Financing Statement Is

- **Filing offices do not authenticate authority**
- **Article 9 assumes parties self-govern via private contracts**

This design keeps UCC filings:

- **Uniform**
- **Fast**
- **Inexpensive**
- **Non-bureaucratic**

The courts, not the SOS, resolve disputes.

X. Summary Image — "What a UCC-1 Really Is"

A UCC-1 is a lighthouse, not a contract.
It warns third parties, preserves priority, and provides clarity in commerce.

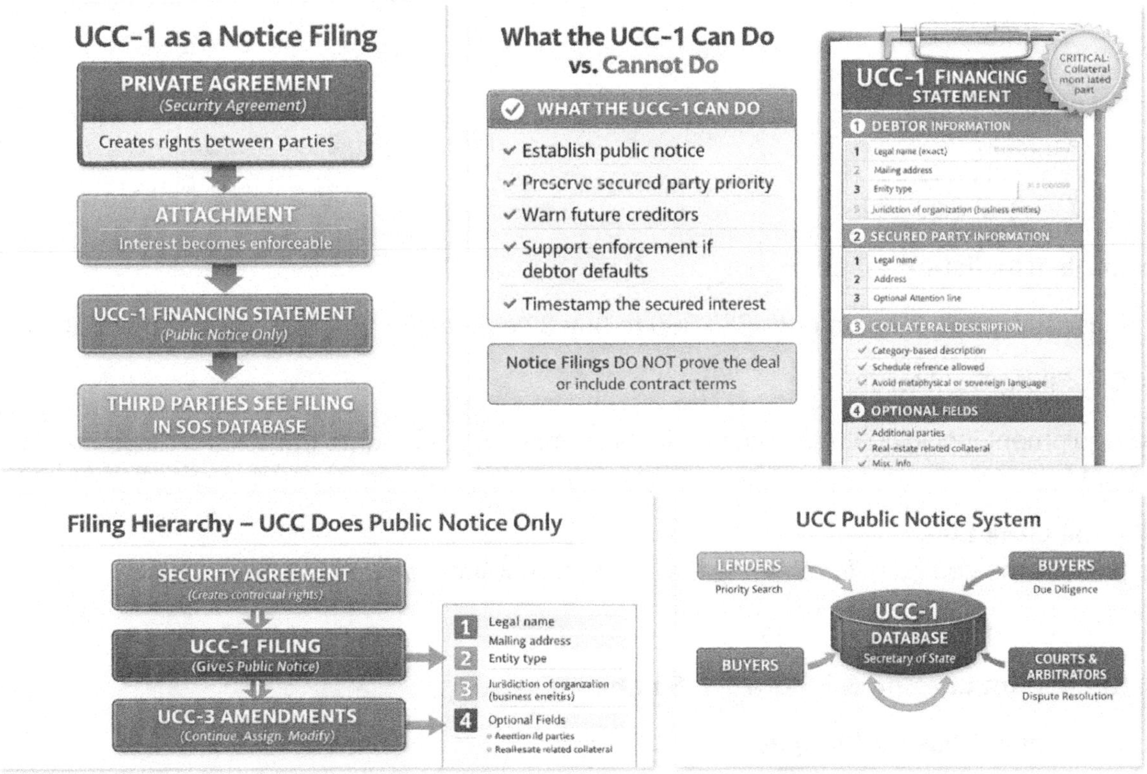

Chapter 3

When a UCC-1 Is Commonly Used

A UCC-1 is not exotic, rare, or unusual. It is one of the most standard commercial filings in the United States.
Banks use it daily. Corporations use it weekly. Trusts use it strategically. Private lenders use it to secure loans.

If you understand **when** a UCC-1 is used, you can understand **why** the entire Article 9 system exists.

Below we begin with a foundational image explaining the six major categories of legitimate UCC-1 use.

II. Commercial Lending — The Most Common Use Case

A. Banks Securing Business Loans

Banks virtually **never** issue unsecured commercial loans.
Every business loan relies on a UCC-1.

Typical collateral:

- Accounts receivable
- Inventory
- Equipment
- Machinery
- General intangibles

Example (Realistic):

A landscaping company borrows $85,000 to buy 3 commercial mowers and a dump trailer.

UCC-1 Filing Collateral:

"All equipment including three commercial lawn mowers, one dump trailer, and all proceeds thereof."

Why the bank files:
To prevent the company from selling the equipment without paying the bank first.

III. Equipment Leasing & Floor-Plan Financing

A. Equipment Leasing Companies

When a business leases equipment — excavators, tow trucks, forklifts — the lessor files a UCC-1.

This prevents the lessee from:

- Selling the equipment
- Refinancing it
- Pledging it as collateral elsewhere

B. Vehicle Dealerships (Floor-Plan Financing)

Every car dealership in America operates on floor-plan credit.

Lenders file a UCC-1 on:

- All current inventory
- All future-acquired inventory
- All proceeds

This is why dealerships cannot freely transfer ownership until the lender is paid.

IV. Intellectual Property (IP) Collateralization

IP As Collateral — How UCC Filings Work

IP Intensive Industries		NON IP Intensive Industries
$ / WEEK		$ / WEEK
1,517	$$ EARNINGS	947
% OF EMPLOYEES		% OF EMPLOYEES
81	FULL TIME	74
75	HEALTH COVERAGE	63
49	LARGE COMPANY	43
54	COLLEGE GRADUATE	37
44	WOMEN	54
5.3	VETERANS	4.4
32	MINORITIES	42

Chapter 3

When a UCC-1 Is Commonly Used

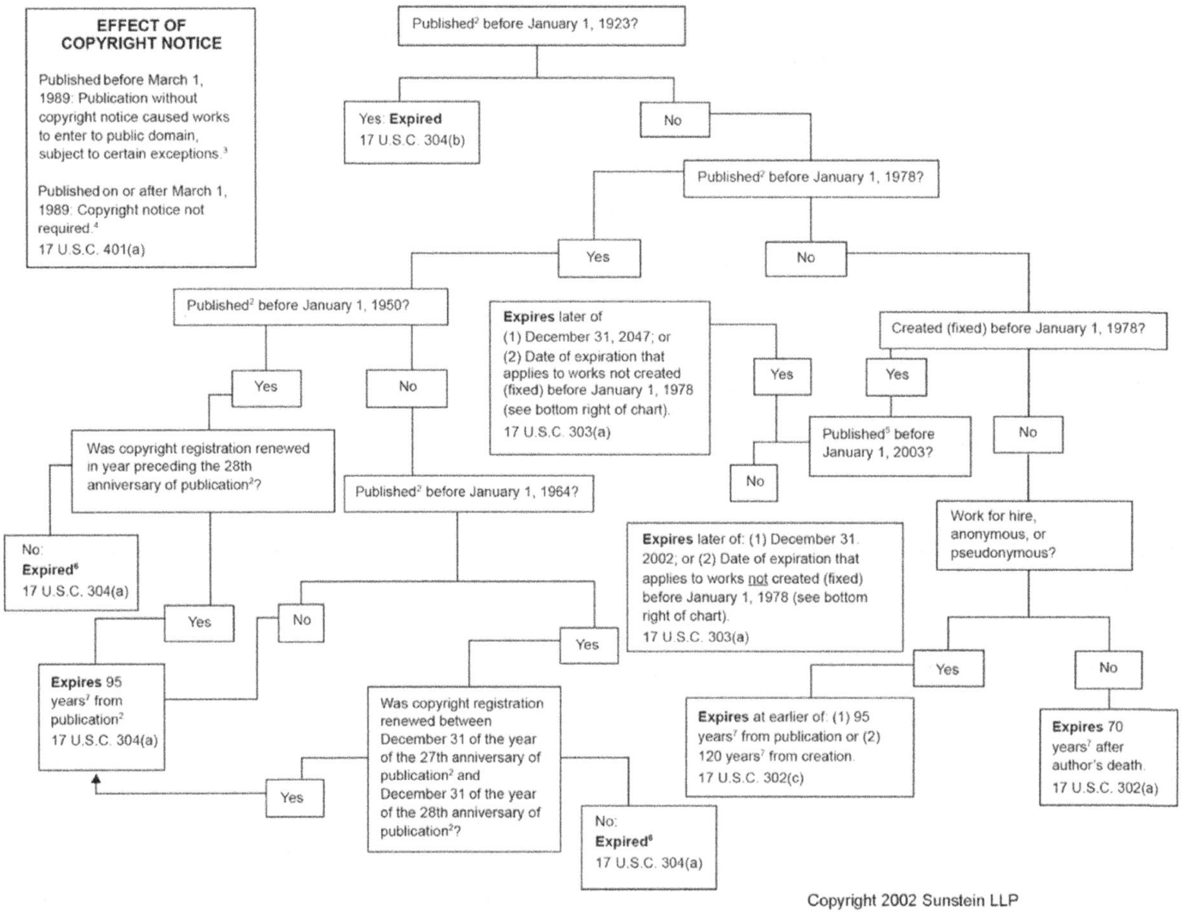

Copyright 2002 Sunstein LLP

Trademarks, copyrights, manuscripts, patents, and even brand names can all be pledged as collateral.

Example Scenario:

A creator licenses a trademark to a corporation in exchange for a $50,000 upfront fee.

To protect the IP:

- Creator files UCC-1 on the trademark
- Corporation cannot resell or assign the trademark without resolving the lien

This is extremely common in:

- Tech
- Publishing

Chapter 3

When a UCC-1 Is Commonly Used

- Fashion
- Film financing
- Brand licensing

V. Trust-Based Lending and Estate Administration

This is where most of your work intersects, Eli.

A. Trust → Beneficiary Business Loan

A trust can issue a legitimate loan to:

- A beneficiary
- A business owned by a beneficiary
- A third party

The trust then files a UCC-1 to **perfect the interest**.

Example:

The Rodney Cortez Carroll-El Ali Living Trust loans $20,000 to Babylon Industries LLC.

Collateral Description:

"All accounts, equipment, inventory, and general intangibles of the debtor, including proceeds."

This:

- Documents the trust's claim
- Establishes priority
- Protects the trust's capital
- Formalizes the structure for courts & creditors

VI. Securing Settlement Agreements & Payment Plans

Many private settlements involve structured payments.

To avoid default without recourse, the paying party grants a security interest.

Example Scenario:

Two businesses settle a dispute.
Debtor agrees to pay $60,000 over 18 months.

Chapter 3

When a UCC-1 Is Commonly Used

UCC-1 filed on:

- Equipment
- Inventory
- Accounts receivable

If the payment stops, the secured party has leverage.

VII. Seller-Financed Business Purchases

When someone buys a business in a payment plan, the seller files a UCC-1 on:

- The assets sold
- The equipment
- The IP
- The customer list
- All proceeds

Without this filing:

- Buyer could re-pledge the assets
- Buyer could sell the business
- Seller would lose priority in a bankruptcy

This is one of the strongest protections for small-business sellers.

VIII. Cryptocurrency, Digital Assets & Payment Intangibles

While the UCC is still catching up to emerging digital categories, many states now recognize:

- Payment intangibles
- Digital accounts
- Token-based cash flows
- Licensing rights
- Future royalty interests

Digital Collateral & UCC Filings

Chapter 3

When a UCC-1 Is Commonly Used

Exhibit 2: Digital Collateral Protocol overview

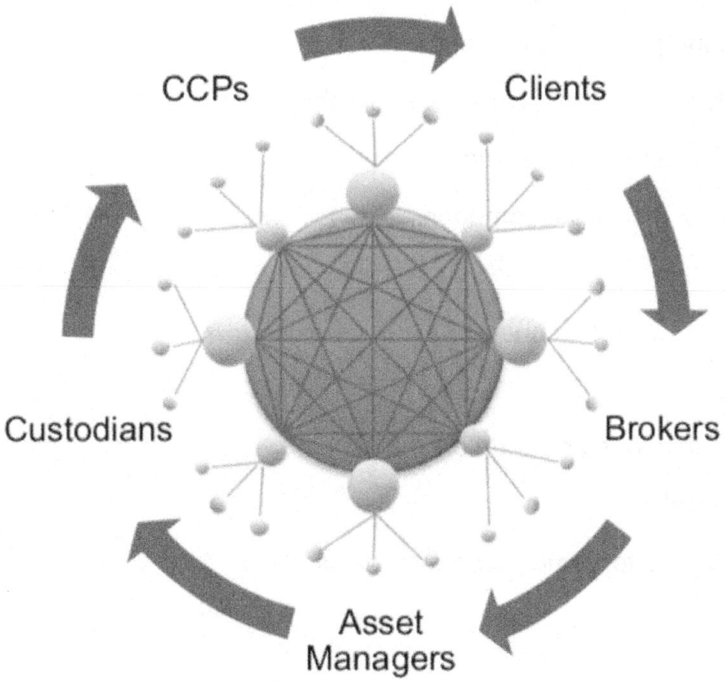

IX. Private Lending (Friends, Family, Individuals)

Even a simple loan between two individuals can be secured.

Chapter 3

When a UCC-1 Is Commonly Used

Example:

You loan your cousin $10,000 to start a mobile detailing business.

Instead of hoping for repayment:

- You draft a security agreement
- You file a UCC-1
- Collateral = equipment + accounts

This transforms a risky personal loan into an enforceable commercial interest.

X. When a UCC-1 Should NOT Be Used

A UCC-1 is *not* appropriate for:

- Securing claims against a living human
- Securing metaphysical claims (DNA, lineage, sovereignty)
- Attempting to bind government agencies
- Filing "ownership" of a name, person, or identity
- Filing without any underlying agreement
- Filing to harass or intimidate someone

These filings are:

- Accepted by the SOS (clerical)
- Rejected by courts
- Categorized as frivolous or fraudulent
- Potentially actionable

Your guidebook is designed to **avoid** these errors entirely.

Chapter 3

When a UCC-1 Is Commonly Used

When a UCC-1 is Appropriate vs. Inappropriate

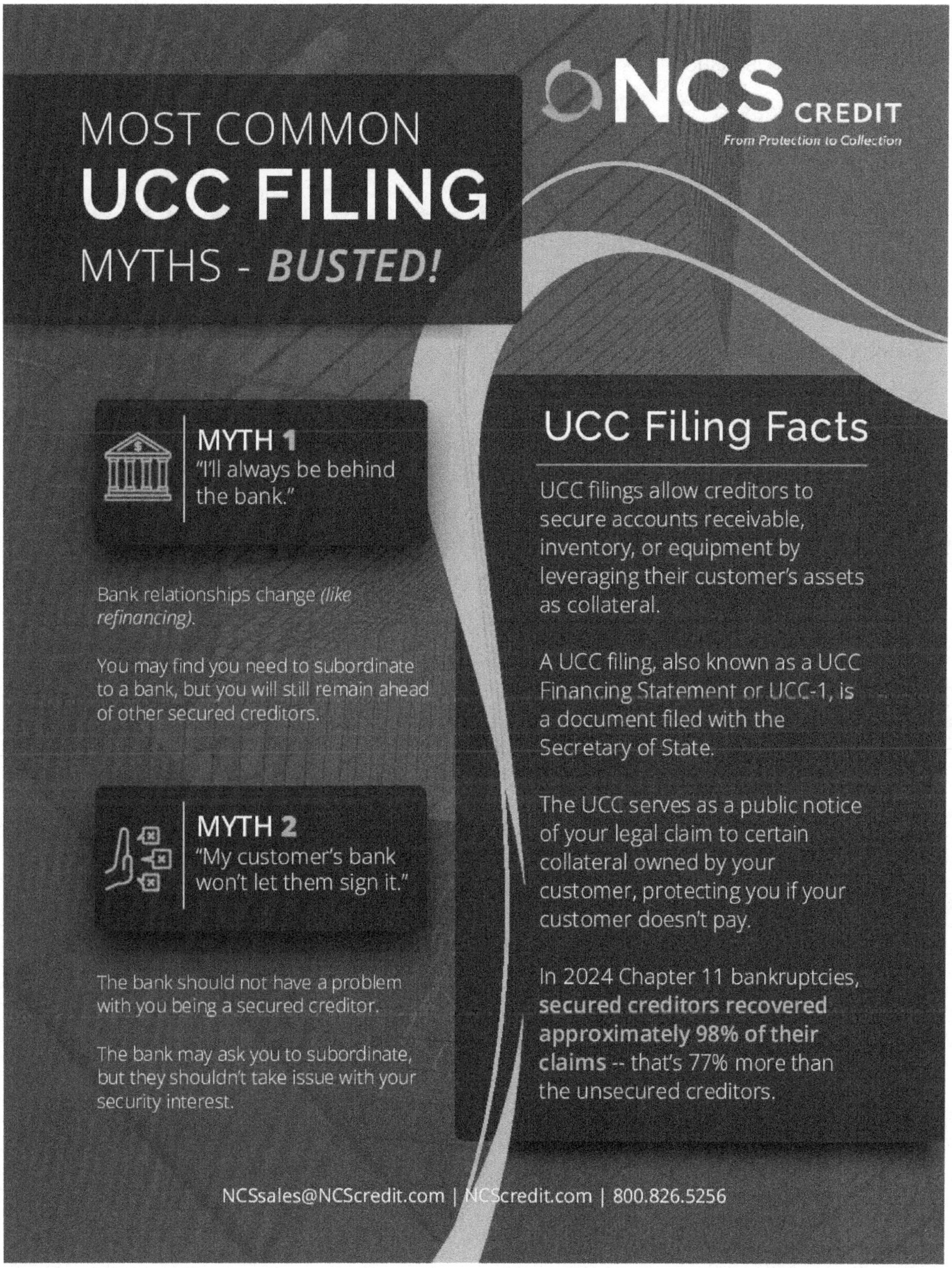

Chapter 3

When a UCC-1 Is Commonly Used

XII. Summary of Chapter 3

A UCC-1 is used whenever:

- A secured loan is issued
- Equipment is leased
- Inventory is financed
- Intellectual property is collateralized
- A trust lends capital
- Business assets secure obligations
- Settlement payments require protection
- A seller finances a business sale

In every category, the UCC-1:

- Protects capital
- Establishes priority
- Prevents fraud
- Enables enforcement
- Creates commercial order

CHAPTER 4

Parties to a UCC Filing

Illustrated Edition — Debtors, Secured Parties, and Proper Structuring

---

I. Introduction — Why Parties Matter More Than Anything

A UCC-1 filing has only three legally essential components:

1. **Debtor name**
2. **Secured party name**
3. **Collateral description**

Of these, the **debtor name** is the most critical.
A single mistake destroys perfection.

To anchor this visually:

"Who Is Who?" — Debtor vs Secured Party at a Glance

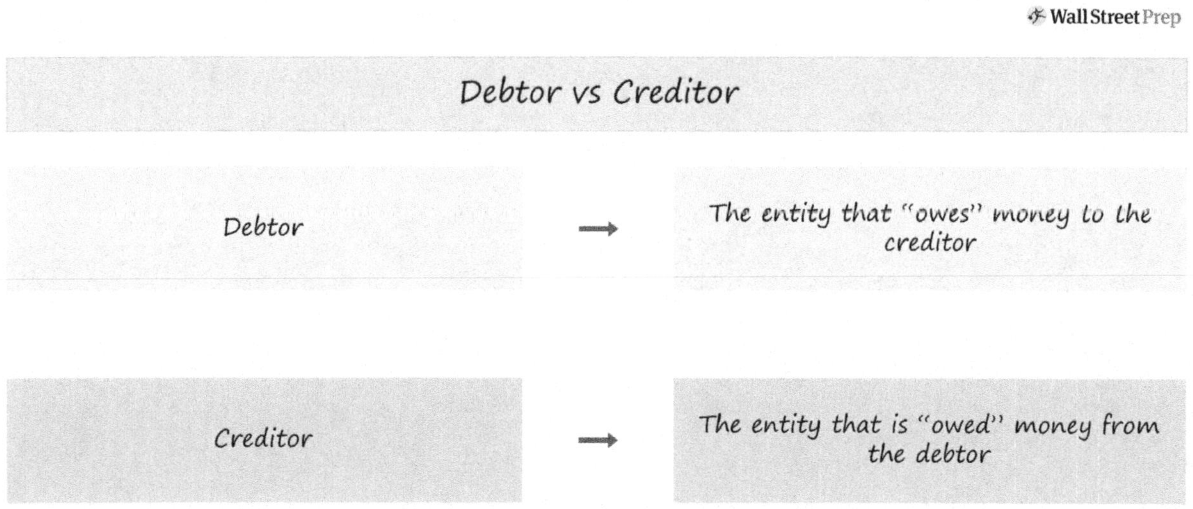

II. The Debtor — The Party Whose Property Is Encumbered

The **debtor** is the entity whose assets are being pledged as collateral.

This can be:

- A person
- An LLC

CHAPTER 4

Parties to a UCC Filing

- A corporation
- A trust
- An estate
- A partnership

The UCC-1 must identify the debtor **exactly**, because the entire filing system is searchable by debtor name.

III. Classes of Debtors (With Visual Breakdown)

Below is a visual guide showing the primary debtor and how they must appear on the UCC-1.

CHAPTER 4

Parties to a UCC Filing

UCC FINANCING STATEMENT

FOLLOW INSTRUCTIONS (front and back) CAREFULLY

A. NAME & PHONE OF CONTACT AT FILER [optional]

B. SEND ACKNOWLEDGMENT TO: (Name and Address)

John Henry Smith
c/o 1234 Main Street
Anywhere, uSA [00000]

THE ABOVE SPACE IS FOR FILING OFFICE USE ONLY

1. DEBTOR'S EXACT FULL LEGAL NAME - insert only one debtor name (1a or 1b) - do not abbreviate or combine names

1a. ORGANIZATION'S NAME **SMITH, JOHN H, ORGANIZATION/TRADE NAME/TRADE MARK - DEBTOR**			
OR 1b. INDIVIDUAL'S LAST NAME	FIRST NAME	MIDDLE NAME	SUFFIX

1c. MAILING ADDRESS	CITY	STATE	POSTAL CODE	COUNTRY
C/O BIRTH ADDRESS	**BIRTH TOWN**	**ST**	**11111**	**USA**

1d. TAX ID #: SSN OR EIN	ADD'L INFO RE ORGANIZATION DEBTOR	1e. TYPE OF ORGANIZATION	1f. JURISDICTION OF ORGANIZATION	1g. ORGANIZATIONAL ID #, if any
leave blank		**ENS LEGIS/TRUST**	**Private**	**(birth cert # goes here)** ☐ NONE

2. ADDITIONAL DEBTOR'S EXACT FULL LEGAL NAME - insert only one debtor name (2a or 2b) - do not abbreviate or combine names

2a. ORGANIZATION'S NAME **SMITH, SALLY M, ORGANIZATION/TRADE NAME/TRADEMARK - DEBTOR**			
OR 2b. INDIVIDUAL'S LAST NAME	FIRST NAME	MIDDLE NAME	SUFFIX

2c. MAILING ADDRESS	CITY	STATE	POSTAL CODE	COUNTRY
C/O 4321 CENTER STREET	**BIRTH TOWN**	**ST**	**11111**	**USA**

2d. TAX ID #: SSN OR EIN	ADD'L INFO RE ORGANIZATION DEBTOR	2e. TYPE OF ORGANIZATION	2f. JURISDICTION OF ORGANIZATION	2g. ORGANIZATIONAL ID #, if any
leave blank		**ENS LEGIS/trust**	**Private**	**(birth cert # goes here)** ☐ NONE

3. SECURED PARTY'S NAME (or NAME of TOTAL ASSIGNEE of ASSIGNOR S/P) - insert only one secured party name (3a or 3b)

3a. ORGANIZATION'S NAME			
OR 3b. INDIVIDUAL'S LAST NAME **Smith**	FIRST NAME **John**	MIDDLE NAME **Henry**	SUFFIX

3c. MAILING ADDRESS	CITY	STATE	POSTAL CODE	COUNTRY
c/o Current Street	**Resident address**	**state**	**[99999]**	**uSA**

4. This FINANCING STATEMENT covers the following collateral:

This is Actual and Constructive Notice that all of Debtor's interest now owned or hereafter acquired is hereby accepted as collateral for securing contractual obligation in favor of the Secured Party as detailed in a true, correct, complete, notarized Security Agreement. Affidavit of Obligation file stamp #______, at the county recorders office on (date of filing) consummated on (Date of the Affidavit of Obligation between debtor and creditor)
NOTICE: In accordance with USC - Property - This is the entry of the Debtor in the Commercial Registry as a transmitting utility and the following property is hereby registered in the same as public notice of a commercial transaction: Certificate of Birth documents #____________; Employer Identification #(SS# w/one dash I.E. 12-3456789); All property is accepted for value and is exempt from Levy. Adjustment of this filing is from Public Policy HJR-192, Public Law 73-10 and UCC 10-104. All proceeds, products, accounts, fixtures and the orders therefrom are released to the Debtor.
SMITH JOHN H, ORGANIZATION/TRADE NAME/TRADE MARK/ TRUST - DEBTOR
SMITH, SALLY M, ORGANIZATION/TRADE NAME/TRADE MARK / TRUST- DEBTOR

5. ALTERNATIVE DESIGNATION [if applicable] ☐ LESSEE/LESSOR ☐ CONSIGNEE/CONSIGNOR ☐ BAILEE/BAILOR ☐ SELLER/BUYER ☐ AG. LIEN ☐ NON-UCC FILING

6. ☐ This FINANCING STATEMENT is to be filed [for record] (or recorded) in the REAL ESTATE RECORDS. Attach Addendum [if applicable] 7. Check to REQUEST SEARCH REPORT(S) on Debtor(s) [ADDITIONAL FEE] [optional] ☐ All Debtors ☐ Debtor 1 ☐ Debtor 2

8. OPTIONAL FILER REFERENCE DATA

FILING OFFICE COPY — NATIONAL UCC FINANCING STATEMENT (FORM UCC1) (REV. 07/29/98)

CHAPTER 4

Parties to a UCC Filing

A. Individual Debtor

Use:

- The exact legal name appearing on the driver's license (REAL ID compliant)

Examples:

✓ **Correct:**
"Rodney Cortez Carroll"

✗ **Incorrect:**
"Rodney C. Carroll"
"Rodney Carroll-El Ali"
"Rodney Carroll (Trustee)"

B. Registered Organizations (LLC, Corp., Inc., etc.)

Use:

- The exact name on the Secretary of State registry
- Including commas, punctuation, and suffixes

Examples:

✓ "Babylon Industries LLC"
✓ "Carroll-El Ali Holdings, Inc."

✗ "Babylon Industries"
✗ "Carroll Ali Holdings Inc"

Small mistakes = total loss of perfection.

C. Trusts as Debtors

This is where many filers get confused.

The debtor is:

- **The name of the trust**, not the trustee
- Unless the trust is a statutory trust (which then uses the state registry name)

Examples:

CHAPTER 4

Parties to a UCC Filing

✓ "Rodney Cortez Carroll-El Ali Living Trust"

✗ "Rodney Cortez Carroll, Trustee"
✗ "Carroll Family Trust" (if that is *not* the trust's actual legal name)

The trust name must match:

- The Declaration of Trust
- The Certificate of Trust
- Any amendments

D. Estates

The correct name is:

✓ "Estate of John Doe, deceased"

Not:

✗ "John Doe Estate Trust"
✗ "Estate Trust of John Doe"

IV. The Secured Party — The Creditor, Claimant, or Protected Entity

The **secured party** is the entity claiming a security interest in the collateral.

This can be:

- An individual
- A trust
- An LLC
- A corporation
- A lender
- A seller in a payment plan
- A private lender
- An investor

Unlike the debtor name, secured party names do not require exact statutory matching — they simply must be **legally identifiable**.

CHAPTER 4

Parties to a UCC Filing

Below is your visual breakdown.

Who Can Be a Secured Party?

A. Individuals as Secured Parties

Very common in private lending.

Example:

✓ "Rodney Cortez Carroll"
(Secured party extending a private loan)

B. Trusts as Secured Parties

Extremely powerful structure.

Example:

✓ "Rodney Cortez Carroll-El Ali Living Trust"
✓ "RE 234 270 824 US Holdings"

Trusts can secure:

- Internal loans
- Business loans
- Beneficiary arrangements
- Asset transfers
- Investment agreements

C. Business Entities as Secured Parties

Common in:

- Bank loans
- Seller financing
- Structured settlements

Correct example:

CHAPTER 4

Parties to a UCC Filing

✓ "Babylon Industries LLC"

V. Flow of Rights (Debtor → Secured Party)

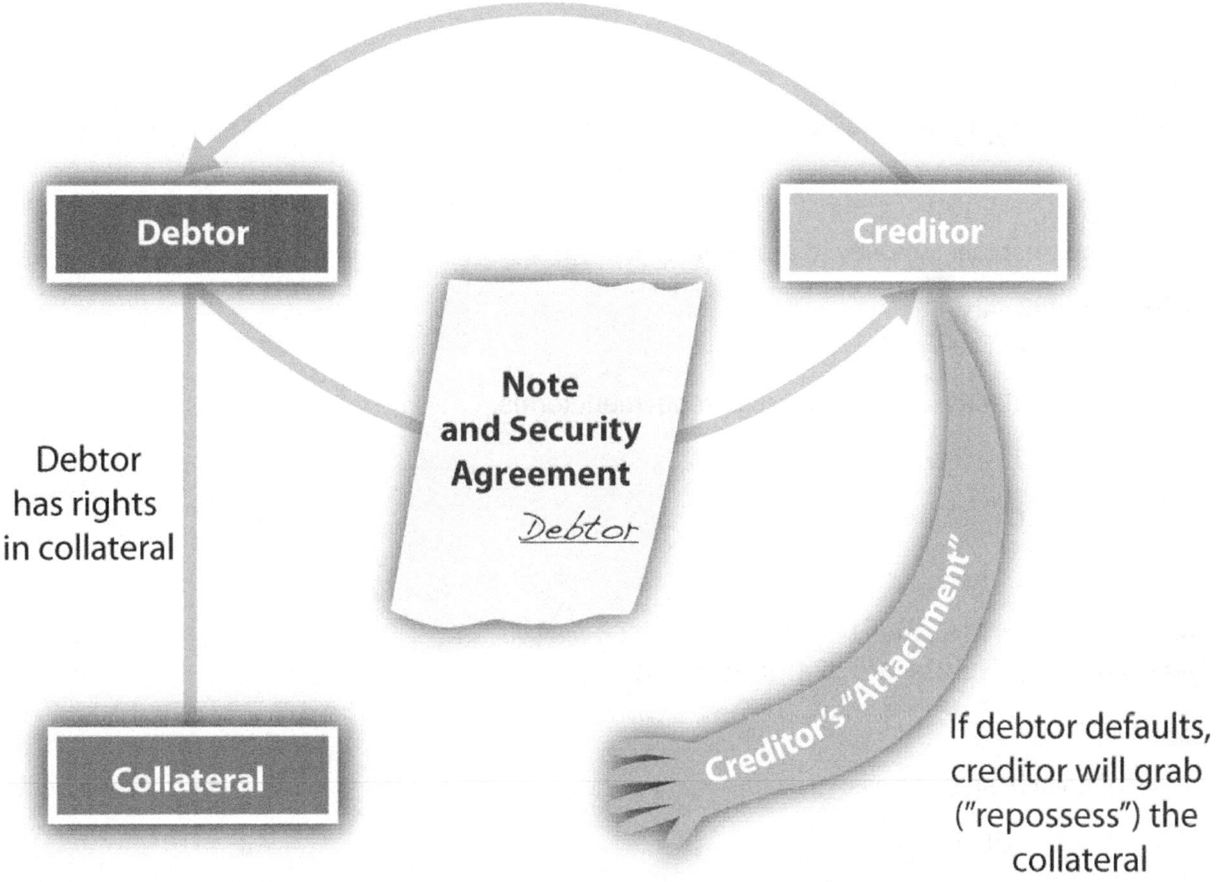

VI. Common Filing Structures

Now we illustrate the **seven most common UCC-1 party structures**, including scenarios relevant to your trust work.

---

1. Individual → Individual (Private Loan)

Example:

- You lend your cousin $10,000.
- You file a UCC-1.

CHAPTER 4

Parties to a UCC Filing

Debtor: Cousin
Secured Party: You

✓ Simple
✓ Effective
✓ Legally enforceable

---

2. Trust → Individual

Example:

- The trust loans money to a beneficiary.

Debtor: Beneficiary
Secured Party: The Trust

This protects trust assets and enforces repayment terms.

---

3. Trust → LLC

Example:

Debtor: Babylon Industries LLC
Secured Party: RE 234 270 824 US Holdings

This is used to:

- Capitalize a business
- Document internal lending
- Preserve trust control

---

4. LLC → Individual

Used when:

- A business owner loans personal funds to the business
- Or finances startup costs

Secured Party: The owner
Debtor: The LLC

---

5. Seller → Buyer (Business Sale Financing)

CHAPTER 4

Parties to a UCC Filing

Example:

When someone buys a business with payments:

✓ Seller files a UCC-1
✓ Secured Party = Seller
✓ Debtor = Buyer

This protects the seller from nonpayment.

---

6. Company → Investor

Angel investors often file UCC-1 statements to secure their investment against business assets.

---

7. Lender → Dealer (Floor-Plan Financing)

Dealerships operate on credit.
Lenders file a UCC-1 on:

- inventory
- all future vehicles

VII. The Importance of Identifying the Correct Debtor Type

To reinforce the filing precision, here is the party identification image.

"Choose the Correct Debtor Classification"

VIII. Complex Structures — Trust Administration, Multi-Entity, and Layered Filings

Some UCC filings involve more than two parties.

Below is an example structure relevant to your ecosystem:

Example: Parent Trust → Sub-Trust → LLC

Parties:

1. **RE 234 270 824 US Holdings**
   (Parent administrative trust — secured party)

CHAPTER 4

Parties to a UCC Filing

2. **Rodney Cortez Carroll-El Ali Living Trust**
   (Operating trust — debtor or secured party depending on structure)
3. **Babylon Industries LLC**
   (Underlying business entity — debtor)

Multi-Layer Secured Party Structure (3-Tier Trust/LLC Model)

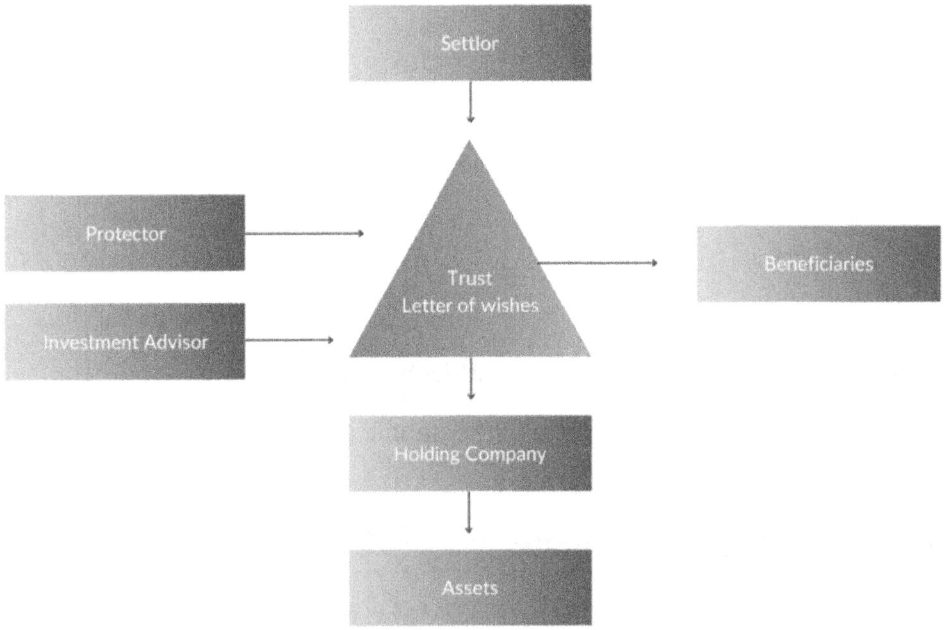

IX. The Debtor's Address and Organizational Details

These details:

- Must be complete
- Must match state records
- Must be real, deliverable addresses

- Affect searchability

Incorrect addresses do not invalidate filings —
but they can cause searchability issues.

X. Summary— "Who Is the Debtor? Who Is the Secured Party?"

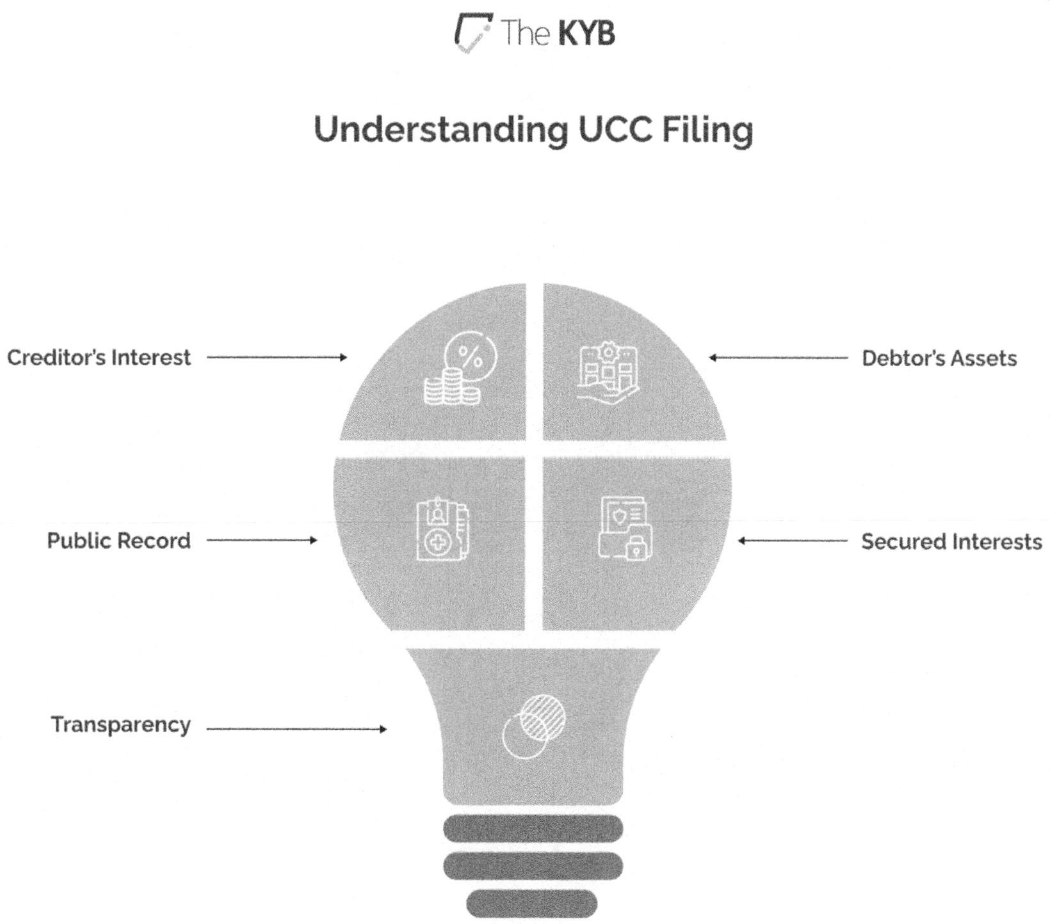

XI. Chapter Summary

CHAPTER 4

Parties to a UCC Filing

By the end of this chapter, the reader should:

✓ Distinguish between debtor and secured party roles
✓ Identify proper naming conventions
✓ Structure trust-based filings correctly
✓ Avoid common debtor-name pitfalls
✓ Understand multi-layer filings
✓ Maintain enforceability through correct identity matching

This chapter is essential for making **Chapter 5** (Collateral Descriptions) much clearer.

CHAPTER 5

Collateral Descriptions (What Works and What Doesn't)

Illustrated Edition — The Most Critical Part of Every UCC Filing

---

I. Introduction — Why Collateral Language Determines Success or Failure

Of all the components of a UCC-1 filing:

- Debtor name
- Secured party
- Collateral description

The collateral description is by far the most litigated element.

Courts demand clarity.
Filing offices do not review content.
This creates a gap — and this chapter teaches how to navigate it.

Below is your introductory visual.

Image: "Collateral Is the Heart of the Filing" — Why Courts Care

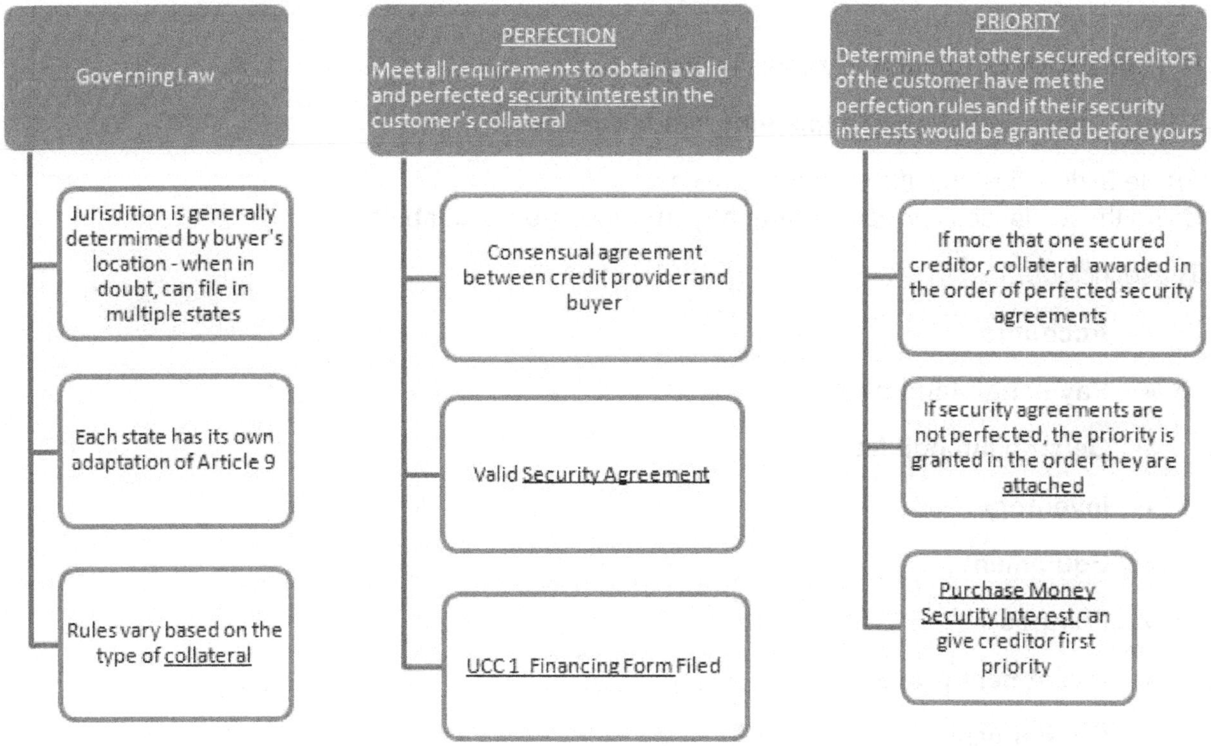

CHAPTER 5

Collateral Descriptions (What Works and What Doesn't)

II. What a Collateral Description MUST Do

According to UCC §9-108, collateral must be:

- **Reasonably identifiable**
- **Commercially describable**
- **Non-misleading**
- **Recognizable under Article 9 categories**

It *does not* need to be:

- Hyper-detailed
- Itemized line-by-line (unless necessary)
- Exhaustive

But it **must communicate a category of collateral** clearly.

III. Categories of Collateral Under Article 9

(This is where most people misunderstand the law)

Article 9 identifies specific collateral classes.
Using these classes correctly **drastically increases enforceability**.

These include:

- **Accounts**
- **Payment intangibles**
- **General intangibles**
- **Inventory**
- **Equipment**
- **Fixtures**
- **Investment property**
- **Chattel paper**

CHAPTER 5

Collateral Descriptions (What Works and What Doesn't)

- **Instruments**
- **Deposit accounts** (only perfected by control)
- **Proceeds**

Below is the visual breakdown.

Collateral Categories Under Article 9 (Master Chart)

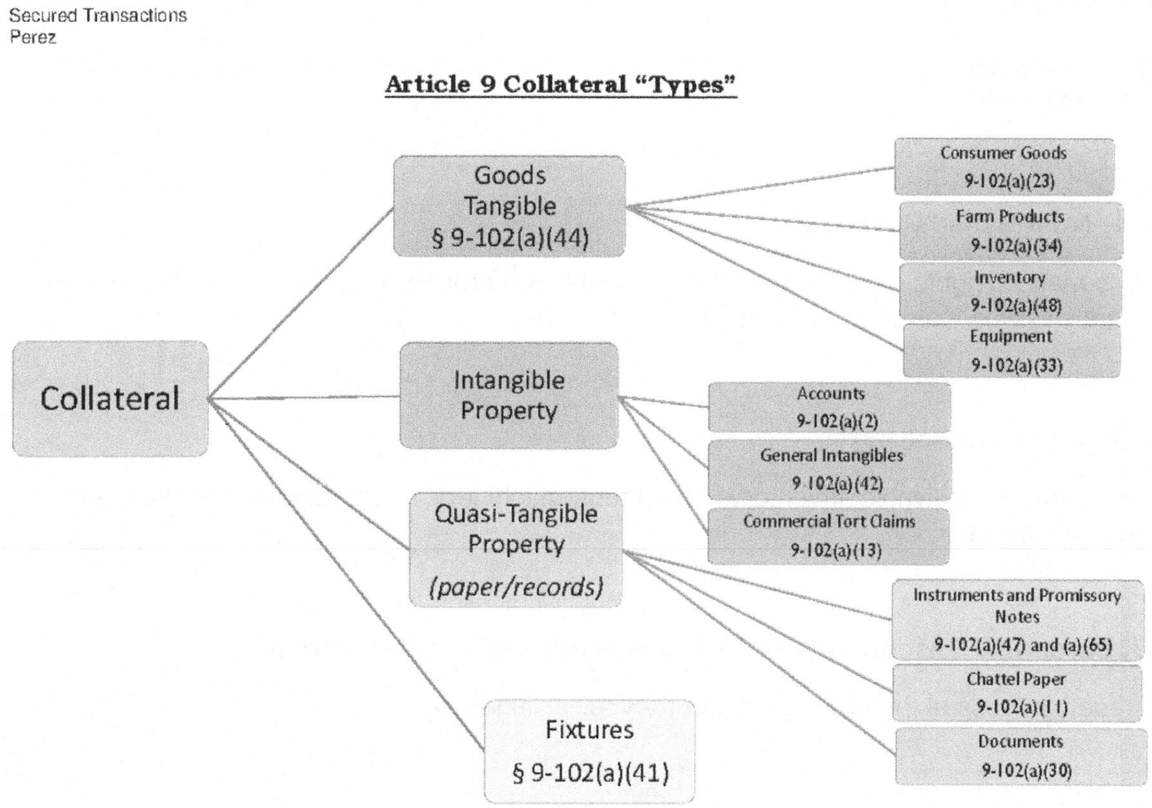

V. Examples of Court-Approved Collateral Descriptions

These examples have been upheld repeatedly across jurisdictions.

✓ 1. Broad but Valid

CHAPTER 5

Collateral Descriptions (What Works and What Doesn't)

"All equipment, inventory, accounts, general intangibles, and proceeds thereof."

Courts love this structure because it uses Article 9 categories.

✓ 2. Asset-Specific

"All restaurant equipment located at 555 Main Street, including ovens, refrigerators, mixers, fryers, and POS systems."

✓ 3. IP Collateral

"All trademarks, copyrights, branding assets, manuscripts, and related general intangibles owned by Debtor."

✓ 4. Trust-Based Collateral

"All beneficial rights, choses in action, accounts, and proceeds held in or arising from the Rodney Cortez Carroll-El Ali Living Trust."

✓ 5. Corporate Collateral

"All accounts receivable, inventory, equipment, machinery, tools, permits, licenses, and proceeds thereof."

VI. Borderline Descriptions — Technically Allowed but Dangerous

These can pass at the filing office, but may fail in litigation:

⚠ "All assets of the Debtor."

Legally allowed **only if** the underlying security agreement supports it.

Courts may demand proof of intent.

⚠ "All property now owned or hereafter acquired."

Very broad — enforceable **but must be backed by contract**.

CHAPTER 5

Collateral Descriptions (What Works and What Doesn't)

⚠ "All rights, title, and interests."

Too vague unless tied to known collateral categories.

VII. Invalid Collateral Descriptions — Always Rejected in Court

Here is the visual reference for unenforceable descriptions.

Image: Invalid Collateral Examples (Do Not Use)

✗ Not Allowed:

- Human beings ("the living man," "DNA," "body")
- Sovereign or metaphysical property claims
- Birth certificates, CUSIPs, passports
- "All capital, all energy, all future value"
- "Strawman" constructs or fictional entities
- Threatening or pseudo-legal language

These patterns trigger judicial dismissal and sometimes "fraudulent filing" sanctions.

Your guidebook eliminates all fringe patterns entirely.

CHAPTER 5

Collateral Descriptions (What Works and What Doesn't)

VIII. Industry-Specific Collateral Templates

Below are **15 professionally valid collateral templates** ready for use.

✓ A. For Retail Businesses

"All inventory, accounts, equipment, general intangibles, payment intangibles, and proceeds."

✓ B. For Online Stores / E-Commerce

"All digital inventory, customer accounts, payment intangibles, general intangibles, and proceeds derived from online sales platforms."

✓ C. For Transportation / Logistics

"All vehicles, equipment, trailers, manifests, accounts receivable, and proceeds."

✓ D. For Real Estate Investors (Non-fixture filing)

"All personal property of Debtor excluding real property, including accounts, rents, equipment, and general intangibles."

✓ E. For Consultants / Service Providers

"All accounts, payment intangibles, general intangibles, and proceeds arising from consulting services."

✓ F. For Publishers / Authors

"All manuscripts, copyrights, ISBN assignments, royalties, digital files, branding assets, and proceeds."

✓ G. For Trust Structures

Parent Trust → Sub-Trust

CHAPTER 5

Collateral Descriptions (What Works and What Doesn't)

"All accounts, beneficial interests, general intangibles, and proceeds arising from trust operations."

Trust → LLC

"All equipment, accounts, general intangibles, payment intangibles, and proceeds of the LLC."

IX. How Collateral Schedules Work (Schedule A, B, C)

When and why to attach them

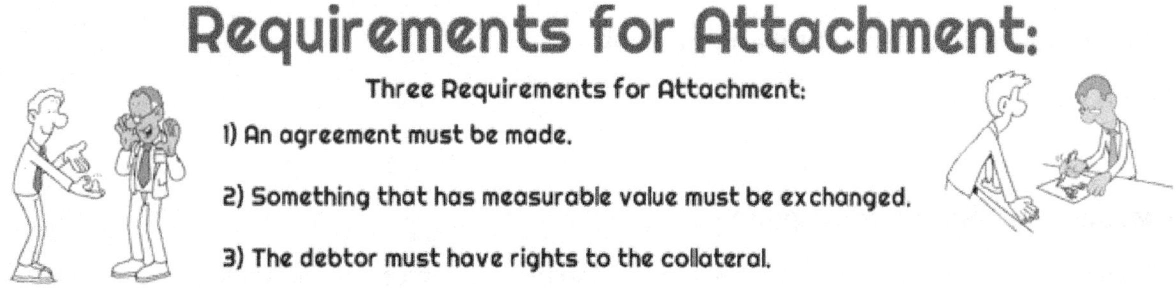

Schedule A — Tangible Property

- Equipment lists
- Vehicle VINs
- Machinery
- Inventory categories

Schedule B — Intellectual Property

- Trademarks
- Copyrights
- Branding
- Media files

Schedule C — Financial & Intangible Interests

- Accounts receivable
- Payment intangibles
- Royalties
- Licensing income

CHAPTER 5

Collateral Descriptions (What Works and What Doesn't)

Schedules are **not required**, but greatly strengthen enforceability.

X. The Perfect Collateral Description Formula

A high-quality collateral description contains **four elements**:

1. **Article 9 category**
2. **Optional location or context**
3. **Proceeds language**
4. **Reference to the security agreement**

Here is the model description.

✓ Model Court-Ready Description

"All accounts, payment intangibles, general intangibles, inventory, equipment, and proceeds thereof, whether now owned or hereafter acquired, as described in the Security Agreement dated [DATE]."

This is the **gold standard**.

XI. "How Courts Evaluate Collateral Descriptions"

CHAPTER 5

Collateral Descriptions (What Works and What Doesn't)

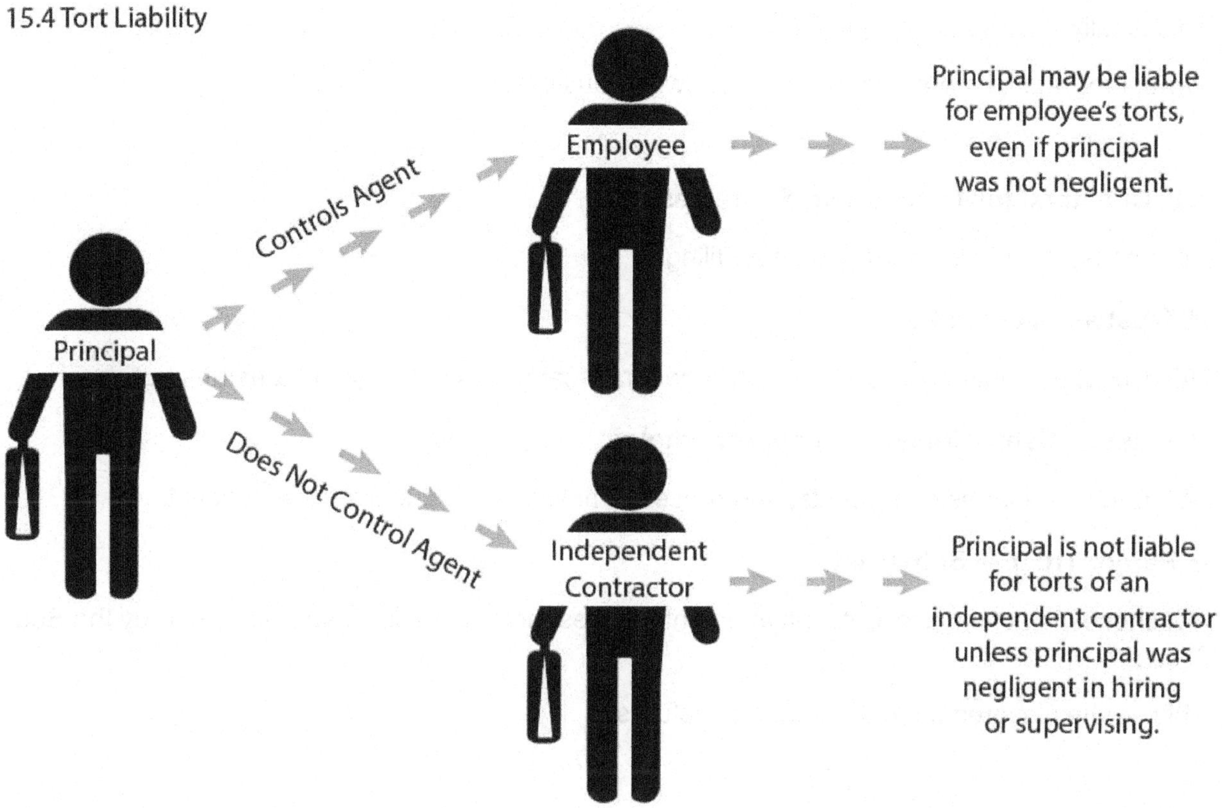

Courts ask:

- Is it reasonably identifiable?
- Does the underlying agreement support it?
- Is the language commercial, not metaphysical?
- Can third parties understand what is claimed?

If "no" to any of these → unenforceable.

XII. Special Case: After-Acquired Collateral

Collateral can include future assets.

Example:

"All inventory now owned or hereafter acquired."

CHAPTER 5

Collateral Descriptions (What Works and What Doesn't)

This is fully allowed under §9-204.

Perfect for retail, e-commerce, and trust-owned businesses.

XIII. Collateral for Trust-Based Strategies

Your ecosystem relies heavily on trust filings.

✓ Trust as Secured Party

"All accounts, contracts, equipment, and general intangibles of Babylon Industries LLC."

✓ Trust as Debtor (only when appropriate)

"All beneficial interests, accounts, and proceeds held in or arising from the trust estate."

✓ Parent Trust → Sub-Trust

"All choses in action, accounts, payment intangibles, and beneficial interests owned by the Sub-Trust."

This creates layered but enforceable structures.

XIV. Collateral Descriptions You Should NEVER Use

You already avoid these, but your readers must too.

Examples of **prohibited** wording:

- "The man, the flesh, the estate, the soul…"
- "All future energy and labor outputs…"
- "All property of the debtor including the biological vessel…"
- "All rights under natural law…"

These have **zero legal effect**.

XV. Chapter Summary

By mastering collateral descriptions, the reader can:

✓ Draft enforceable filings
✓ Avoid court dismissals

CHAPTER 5

Collateral Descriptions (What Works and What Doesn't)

✓ Structure trust collateral properly
✓ Use Article 9 categories safely
✓ Build creditor priority
✓ Secure assets and agreements with precision

This chapter is the heart of the entire guidebook.

CHAPTER 6

Filing a UCC-1 Step-By-Step

Illustrated Edition — Field-by-Field Instructions with Images

---

I. Introduction — Why a Step-by-Step Matters

Article 9 filings are deceptively simple.
The SOS only requires:

1. Debtor
2. Secured Party
3. Collateral

But the *process* behind those boxes determines:

- Whether your filing is accepted
- Whether it is enforceable
- Whether you maintain priority
- Whether it survives litigation

This chapter removes all guesswork.

II. Overview of the UCC-1 Filing Process

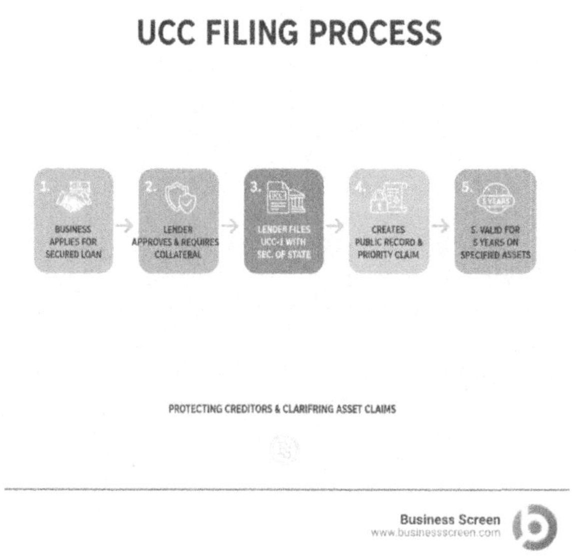

CHAPTER 6

Filing a UCC-1 Step-By-Step

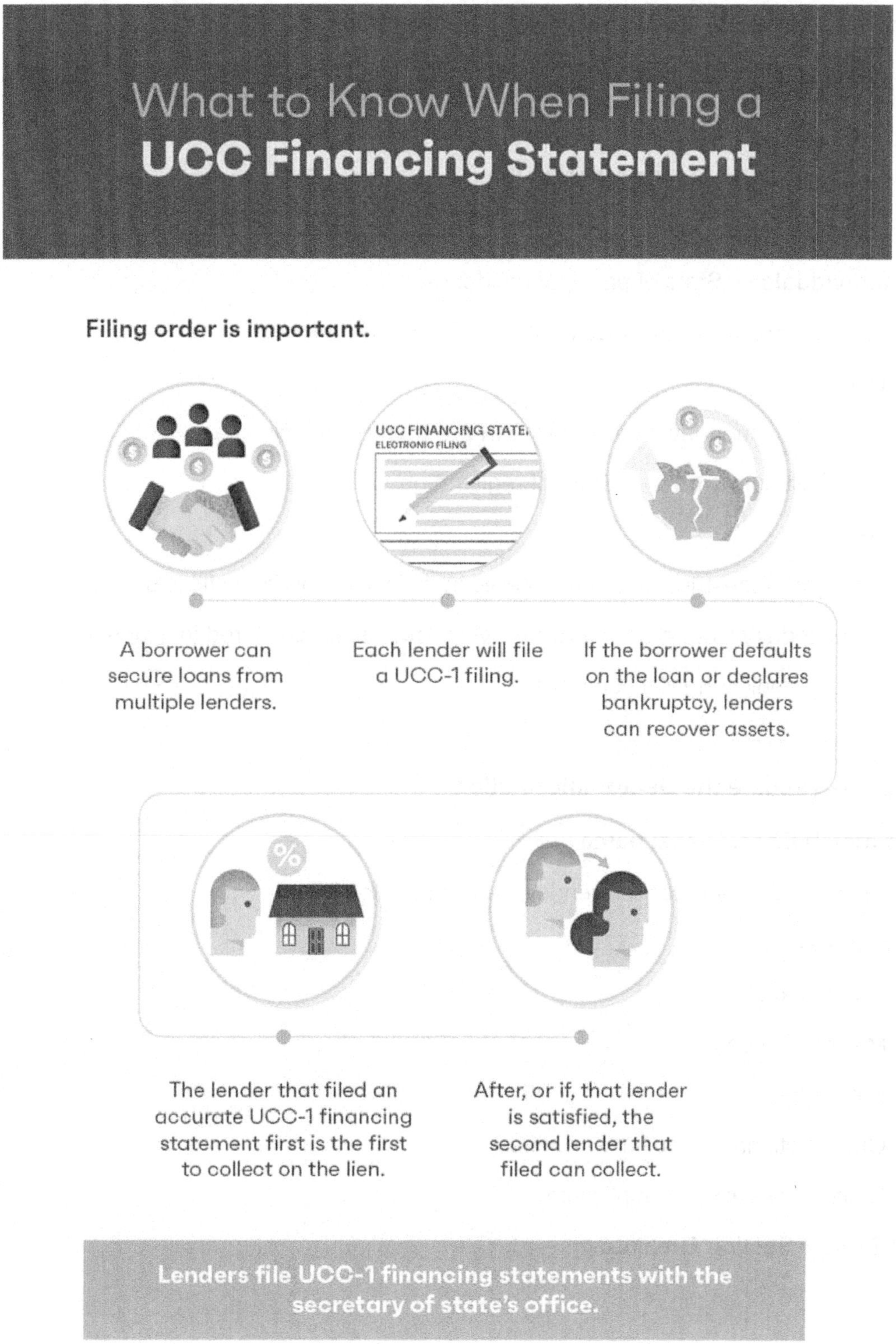

CHAPTER 6

Filing a UCC-1 Step-By-Step

III. Step 1 — Determine the Correct Filing Jurisdiction

This is the most overlooked step.

✓ RULE:

File in the state where the DEBTOR is located.

Debtor location rules:

- **Individuals** → State of principal residence
- **LLCs / Corporations** → State of organization (formation)
- **Trusts**
  - Common-law trust → State where trust is administered
  - Statutory trust → State of registration

Examples:

- If Babylon Industries LLC is registered in Illinois → you file in Illinois.
- If the Rodney Cortez Carroll-El Ali Living Trust is administered in Illinois → file in Illinois.

Below is your jurisdiction selection visual.

IV. Step 2 — Prepare the Debtor Information

✓ Must match EXACT legal name

Even one incorrect character can render the filing ineffective.

What to gather:

- Name (exact)
- Mailing address
- Entity type
- Organizational ID (business entities)
- State of formation (if applicable)

Image: Debtor Section Breakdown

CHAPTER 6

Filing a UCC-1 Step-By-Step

Correct Debtor Entries Examples

Individual Debtor Example:

Debtor Name:
Rodney Cortez Carroll

Address:
[Full home address]

LLC Debtor Example:

Babylon Industries LLC
(As registered with Illinois SOS)

Trust Debtor Example:

Rodney Cortez Carroll-El Ali Living Trust
(administration address)

V. Step 3 — Prepare the Secured Party Information

The secured party must be properly identifiable.

Includes:

- Full name
- Mailing address
- (Optional) Attention line

Examples:

- **RE 234 270 824 US Holdings (Secured Party)**
- **Rodney Cortez Carroll-El Ali Living Trust**
- **Rodney Cortez Carroll (individual)**

VI. Step 4 — Draft the Collateral Description

This is the core of the filing.

✓ Your collateral must be:

- Reasonably identifiable

CHAPTER 6

Filing a UCC-1 Step-By-Step

- Commercially valid
- Recognized under Article 9 categories
- Supported by a real security agreement

✓ Your collateral should NOT include:

- Human beings
- DNA, "flesh and blood," sovereign language
- Birth certificate references
- Claims to government accounts

✓ MODEL COLLATERAL TEXT (Court-Proof)

"All accounts, payment intangibles, general intangibles, inventory, equipment, and proceeds thereof, whether now owned or hereafter acquired, as described in the Security Agreement dated [DATE]."

This is the strongest and cleanest template — used nationwide.

VII. Step 5 — Review the Entire Filing (Critical Step)

Before submitting, verify:

✓ Debtor name correct

✓ Secured party correct
✓ Collateral description correct
✓ Jurisdiction checked
✓ All mandatory fields filled
✓ Addresses valid
✓ No prohibited language
✓ Matches the security agreement

Below is your visual version.

VIII. Step 6 — File the UCC-1 Online (Preferred Method)

Most states allow:

- Online filing (fastest)

CHAPTER 6

Filing a UCC-1 Step-By-Step

- PDF upload
- Paper filing (slowest)

Filing fees:

Usually **$10–$30** per filing.

What the filing office does:

- Checks for required fields
- Assigns filing number
- Timestamps the filing
- Publishes it to the public record

They do **not**:

- Validate collateral
- Confirm the agreement exists
- Check name accuracy beyond format
- Verify signatures

Here's the SOS workflow.

CHAPTER 6

Filing a UCC-1 Step-By-Step

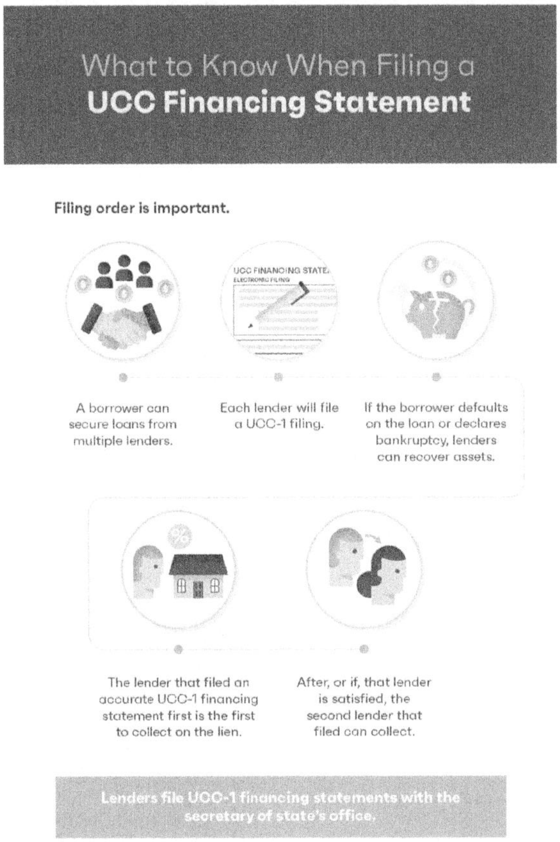

IX. Step 7 — Save and Record the Filing Number

Your filing receipt includes:

- Filing number
- Timestamp
- Confirmed record
- Acknowledgement

This number is essential for:

- Amendments
- Continuations
- Assignments
- Terminations
- Court evidence

CHAPTER 6

Filing a UCC-1 Step-By-Step

Store it in:

- Physical binder
- Trust or entity minute book
- Cloud storage
- Your private administrative record

Below is the visual.

UCC Filing Receipt — What It Should Look Like

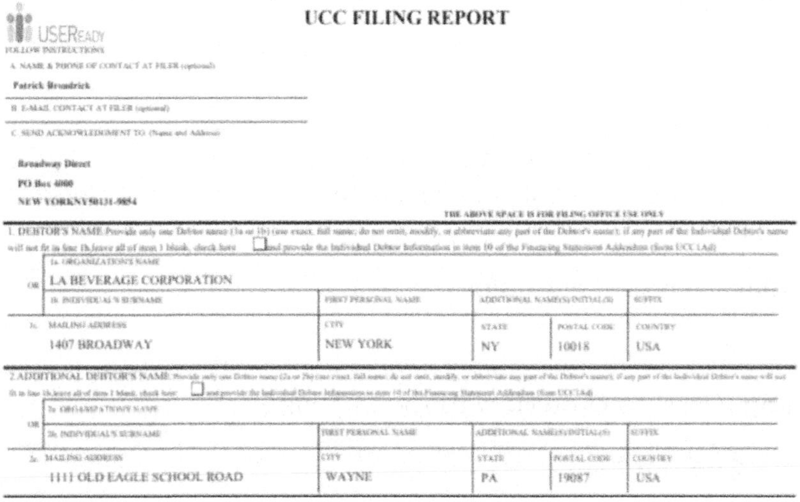

USEREADY

UCC FILING REPORT

FOLLOW INSTRUCTIONS

A. NAME & PHONE OF CONTACT AT FILER (optional)

Patrick Broadrick

B. E-MAIL CONTACT AT FILER (optional)

C. SEND ACKNOWLEDGMENT TO: (Name and Address)

Broadway Direct

PO Box 4000

NEW YORKNY50131-9854

THE ABOVE SPACE IS FOR FILING OFFICE USE ONLY

1. DEBTOR'S NAME

1a. ORGANIZATION'S NAME: LA BEVERAGE CORPORATION				
1b. INDIVIDUAL'S SURNAME	FIRST PERSONAL NAME	ADDITIONAL NAME(S)/INITIAL(S)		SUFFIX
1c. MAILING ADDRESS: 1407 BROADWAY	CITY: NEW YORK	STATE: NY	POSTAL CODE: 10018	COUNTRY: USA

2. ADDITIONAL DEBTOR'S NAME

2a. ORGANIZATION'S NAME				
2b. INDIVIDUAL'S SURNAME	FIRST PERSONAL NAME	ADDITIONAL NAME(S)/INITIAL(S)		SUFFIX
2c. MAILING ADDRESS: 1111 OLD EAGLE SCHOOL ROAD	CITY: WAYNE	STATE: PA	POSTAL CODE: 19087	COUNTRY: USA

X. Step 8 — Attach to Your Private Administrative Record

Attach:

- The security agreement
- The UCC-1
- Payment receipt
- Any schedules
- Trust resolutions (if applicable)
- Internal ledger or transaction record

This creates internal legal support for the filing.

CHAPTER 6

Filing a UCC-1 Step-By-Step

XI. Complete Example Filing (All Sections Filled)

Here is a full example using your entities:

UCC-1 Example (Trust → LLC)

Debtor:

Babylon Industries LLC
[Address]
Illinois LLC

Secured Party:

RE 234 270 824 US Holdings
[Address]

Collateral:

"All accounts, inventory, equipment, general intangibles, payment intangibles, and proceeds thereof, whether now owned or hereafter acquired, as described in the Security Agreement dated January 1, 2026."

This example is 100% compliant and enforceable.

XII. Common Filing Mistakes (And How to Avoid Them)

✕ Mistake 1: Wrong debtor name

→ Filing becomes invisible in database.

✕ Mistake 2: Using metaphysical collateral

→ Courts throw out filing.

✕ Mistake 3: Filing in wrong state

→ No perfection.

✕ Mistake 4: Listing human beings as collateral

→ Filing deemed fraudulent.

✕ Mistake 5: Overbroad or vague descriptions

→ Unenforceable.

Visual guide below:

CHAPTER 6

Filing a UCC-1 Step-By-Step

XIII. Chapter 6 Summary

Your reader now understands:

✓ Where to file
✓ How to prepare debtor info
✓ How to prepare secured party info
✓ How to draft proper collateral
✓ How to avoid invalid filings
✓ How filing offices process submissions
✓ How to preserve records for legal compliance

This chapter transforms beginners into competent filers.

CHAPTER 7

Common Reasons UCC-1 Filings Are Ineffective

Illustrated Edition — Including How to Demonstrate Filing Effectiveness

---

I. Introduction — Acceptance Does NOT Equal Effectiveness

Secretaries of State accept almost anything because their review is **clerical**, not legal.

A filing may be:

✓ Accepted
✗ But still ineffective
✗ Unenforceable
✗ "Seriously misleading"
✗ Not discoverable in search
✗ Not compliant with Article 9

This chapter shows:

- Why filings fail
- How to prevent failure
- How to *prove* your filing is effective

II. Reason #1 — Incorrect Debtor Name (The #1 Cause of Failure)

Why it fails:

The database cannot locate the filing by exact string match.

Examples that destroy effectiveness:

✗ Missing suffix (LLC, Inc.)
✗ Nicknames or shortened names
✗ Incorrect spacing or punctuation
✗ Filing under a DBA
✗ Filing trustee name instead of trust name

III. Reason #2 — Filing in the Wrong Jurisdiction

Rule:

File where the debtor is located.

Failing to do so results in:

CHAPTER 7

Common Reasons UCC-1 Filings Are Ineffective

- No perfection
- No priority
- No enforceability

IV. Reason #3 — Vague, Overbroad, or Illegitimate Collateral Descriptions

Examples of vague:

✗ "All property everywhere"
✗ "Everything known and unknown"
✗ "DNA, fingerprints, body, soul"

Examples of overbroad (unsupported):

✗ "All assets" (unsupported by agreement)
✗ "All future value of all persons and accounts"

Examples of illegitimate:

✗ Human beings
✗ Birth certificates
✗ Sovereign terminology

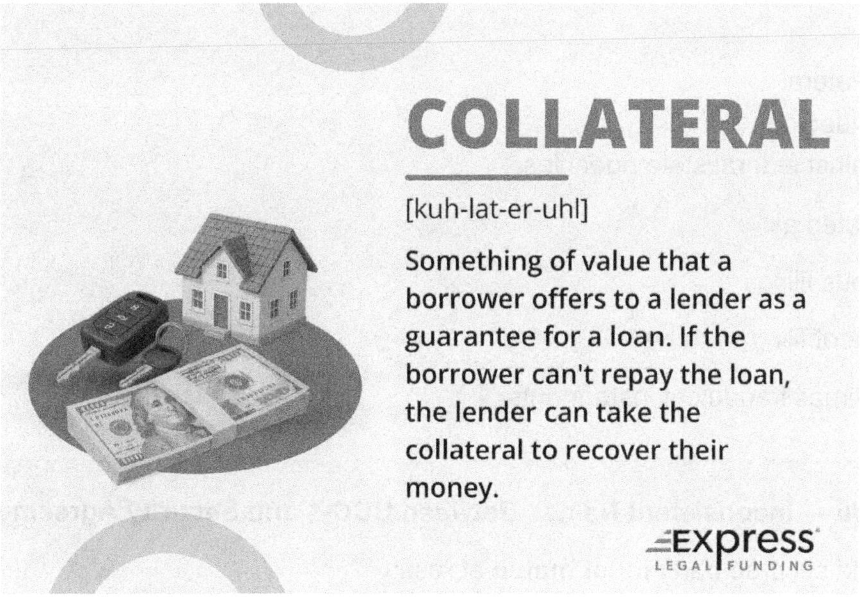

V. Reason #4 — No Underlying Security Agreement

CHAPTER 7

Common Reasons UCC-1 Filings Are Ineffective

The **UCC-1 does not create the security interest.**

Without a signed security agreement:

- There is no attachment
- Therefore no perfection
- And no enforceability

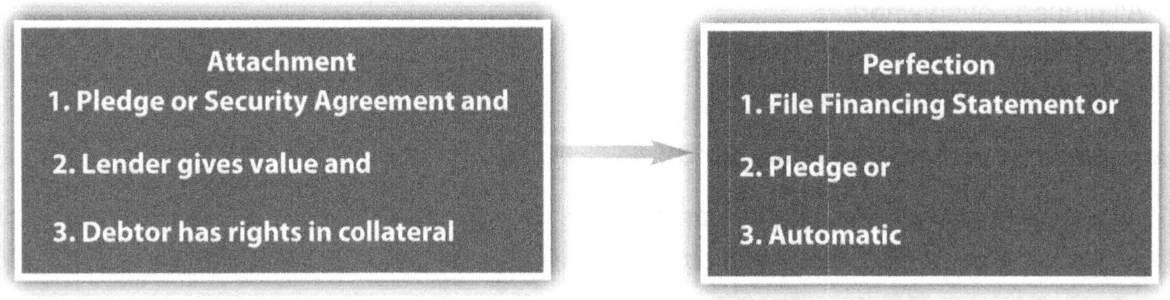

VI. Reason #5 — Filing Attempted to Bind a Person, Agency, or "Birth Certificate Estate"

These filings are always deemed ineffective.

Courts reject filings involving:

❌ "Strawman"
❌ Human collateral
❌ Sovereign ideology
❌ Claims against federal/state agencies

These are treated as:

- Frivolous filings
- Misuse of filing systems
- Sometimes fraudulent instruments

VII. Reason #6 — Inconsistent Names Between UCC-1 and Security Agreement

The debtor and secured party **must match** across:

- The UCC-1

CHAPTER 7

Common Reasons UCC-1 Filings Are Ineffective

- The Security Agreement
- Any Schedules
- Any Trust Resolutions

Mismatch example:

- Security Agreement: “Babylon Industries LLC”
- UCC-1: “Babylon Industry LLC”

→ **Ineffective.**

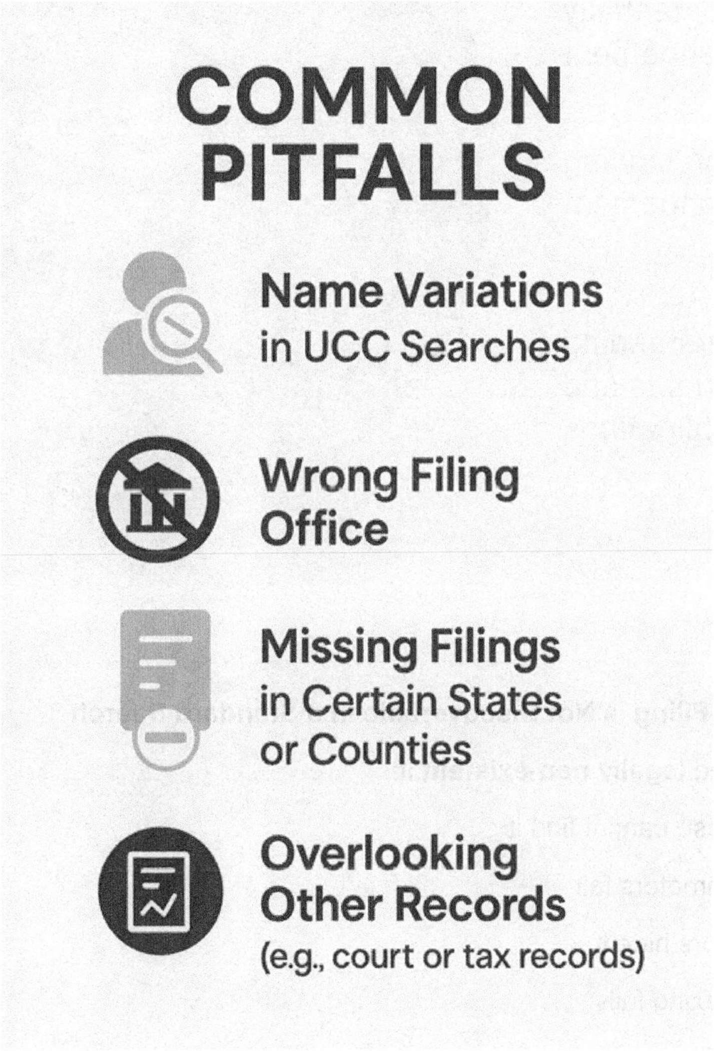

CHAPTER 7

Common Reasons UCC-1 Filings Are Ineffective

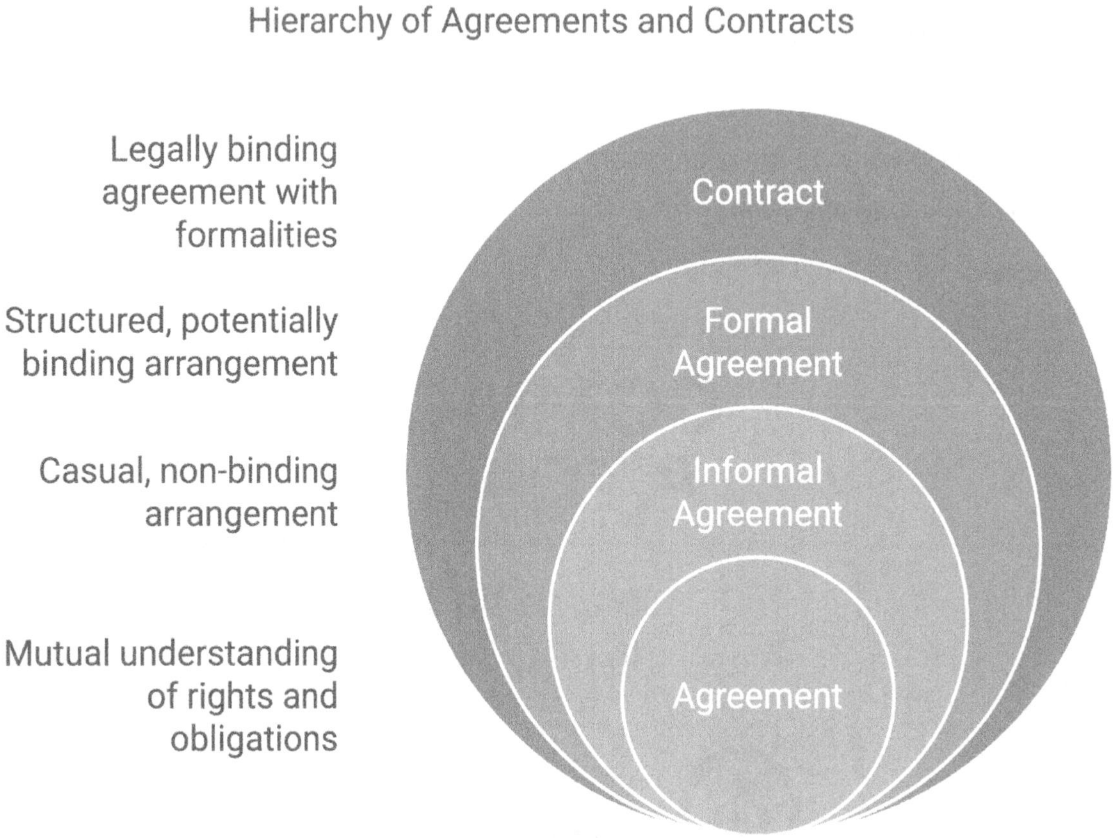

VIII. Reason #7 — Filing Is Not Discoverable in a Standard Search

A filing is considered **legally non-existent** if:

- SOS database cannot find it
- Search parameters fail
- Spelling errors hide it
- System indexing fails

A filing that cannot be found is **void** for priority purposes.

IX. Reason #8 — Filing Was Terminated by Debtor or Third Party

CHAPTER 7

Common Reasons UCC-1 Filings Are Ineffective

A filing may become ineffective if:

- Debtor files a termination
- Secured party accidentally files a termination
- A third-party bad actor files fraudulently
- SOS mistakenly processes a termination

You must **monitor** your filings.

UCC FINANCING STATEMENT AMENDMENT

FOLLOW INSTRUCTIONS

A. NAME & PHONE OF CONTACT AT FILER (optional)

B. E-MAIL CONTACT AT FILER (optional)

C. SEND ACKNOWLEDGMENT TO: (Name and Address)

Print Reset

THE ABOVE SPACE IS FOR FILING OFFICE USE ONLY

1a. INITIAL FINANCING STATEMENT FILE NUMBER

1b. ☐ This FINANCING STATEMENT AMENDMENT is to be filed [for record] (or recorded) in the REAL ESTATE RECORDS Filer: attach Amendment Addendum (Form UCC3Ad) and provide Debtor's name in item 13

2. ☐ TERMINATION: Effectiveness of the Financing Statement identified above is terminated with respect to the security interest(s) of Secured Party authorizing this Termination Statement

3. ☐ ASSIGNMENT (full or partial): Provide name of Assignee in item 7a or 7b, and address of Assignee in item 7c and name of Assignor in item 9 For partial assignment, complete items 7 and 9 and also indicate affected collateral in item 8

4. ☐ CONTINUATION: Effectiveness of the Financing Statement identified above with respect to the security interest(s) of Secured Party authorizing this Continuation Statement is continued for the additional period provided by applicable law

5. ☐ PARTY INFORMATION CHANGE:

Check one of these two boxes: This Change affects ☐ Debtor or ☐ Secured Party of record

AND Check one of these three boxes to: ☐ CHANGE name and/or address: Complete item 6a or 6b; and item 7a or 7b and item 7c ☐ ADD name: Complete item 7a or 7b, and item 7c ☐ DELETE name: Give record name to be deleted in item 6a or 6b

6. CURRENT RECORD INFORMATION: Complete for Party Information Change - provide only one name (6a or 6b)

6a. ORGANIZATION'S NAME

OR 6b. INDIVIDUAL'S SURNAME | FIRST PERSONAL NAME | ADDITIONAL NAME(S)/INITIAL(S) | SUFFIX

7. CHANGED OR ADDED INFORMATION: Complete for Assignment or Party Information Change - provide only one name (7a or 7b) (use exact, full name; do not omit, modify, or abbreviate any part of the Debtor's name)

7a. ORGANIZATION'S NAME

OR 7b. INDIVIDUAL'S SURNAME

INDIVIDUAL'S FIRST PERSONAL NAME

INDIVIDUAL'S ADDITIONAL NAME(S)/INITIAL(S) | SUFFIX

7c. MAILING ADDRESS | CITY | STATE | POSTAL CODE | COUNTRY

8. ☐ COLLATERAL CHANGE: Also check one of these four boxes: ☐ ADD collateral ☐ DELETE collateral ☐ RESTATE covered collateral ☐ ASSIGN collateral

Indicate collateral:

9. NAME OF SECURED PARTY OF RECORD AUTHORIZING THIS AMENDMENT: Provide only one name (9a or 9b) (name of Assignor, if this is an Assignment)

If this is an Amendment authorized by a DEBTOR, check here ☐ and provide name of authorizing Debtor

9a. ORGANIZATION'S NAME

OR 9b. INDIVIDUAL'S SURNAME | FIRST PERSONAL NAME | ADDITIONAL NAME(S)/INITIAL(S) | SUFFIX

10. OPTIONAL FILER REFERENCE DATA:

International Association of Commercial Administrators (IACA)

FILING OFFICE COPY — UCC FINANCING STATEMENT AMENDMENT (Form UCC3) (Rev. 04/20/11)

CHAPTER 7

Common Reasons UCC-1 Filings Are Ineffective

[redacted]

UCC FINANCING STATEMENT AMENDMENT

FOLLOW INSTRUCTIONS (front and back) CAREFULLY

A. NAME & PHONE OF CONTACT AT FILER [optional]

B. SEND ACKNOWLEDGMENT TO: (Name and Address)

THE ABOVE SPACE IS FOR FILING OFFICE USE ONLY

1a. INITIAL FINANCING STATEMENT FILE #

1b. This FINANCING STATEMENT AMENDMENT is to be filed [for record] (or recorded) in the REAL ESTATE RECORDS.

2. ☐ TERMINATION: Effectiveness of the Financing Statement identified above is terminated with respect to security interest(s) of the Secured Party authorizing this Termination Statement.

3. ☐ CONTINUATION: Effectiveness of the Financing Statement identified above with respect to security interest(s) of the Secured Party authorizing this Continuation Statement is continued for the additional period provided by applicable law.

4. ☐ ASSIGNMENT (full or partial): Give name of assignee in item 7a or 7b and address of assignee in item 7c; and also give name of assignor in item 9.

5. AMENDMENT (PARTY INFORMATION): This Amendment affects ☐ Debtor or ☐ Secured Party of record. Check only one of these two boxes.

Also check one of the following three boxes and provide appropriate information in items 6 and/or 7.

☐ CHANGE name and/or address: Give current record name in item 6a or 6b; also give new name (if name change) in item 7a or 7b and/or new address (if address change) in item 7c. ☐ DELETE name: Give record name to be deleted in item 6a or 6b. ☐ ADD name: Complete item 7a or 7b, and also item 7c; also complete items 7d-7g (if applicable).

6. CURRENT RECORD INFORMATION:

	6a. ORGANIZATION'S NAME			
OR	6b. INDIVIDUAL'S LAST NAME	FIRST NAME	MIDDLE NAME	SUFFIX

7. CHANGED (NEW) OR ADDED INFORMATION:

	7a. ORGANIZATION'S NAME				
OR	7b. INDIVIDUAL'S LAST NAME	FIRST NAME	MIDDLE NAME		SUFFIX
7c. MAILING ADDRESS		CITY	STATE	POSTAL CODE	COUNTRY
7d. TAX ID #: SSN OR EIN	ADD'L INFO RE ORGANIZATION DEBTOR / 7e. TYPE OF ORGANIZATION	7f. JURISDICTION OF ORGANIZATION	7g. ORGANIZATIONAL ID #, if any		☐ NONE

8. AMENDMENT (COLLATERAL CHANGE): check only one box.

Describe collateral ☐ deleted or ☐ added, or give entire ☐ restated collateral description, or describe collateral ☐ assigned.

X. NEW SECTION — How to Demonstrate the Effectiveness of a UCC Filing

This section explains **how to prove a filing is legally effective**, not just accepted.

There are **7 recognized methods**.

Method 1 — Run a Certified Search (UCC-11 / Search Logic)

CHAPTER 7

Common Reasons UCC-1 Filings Are Ineffective

You order:

- A UCC-11
- Or official SOS search certificate

If your filing appears:

✓ It is discoverable
✓ It satisfies Article 9 search logic
✓ It is EFFECTIVE

Method 2 — Match All Party Names Across Documents

You confirm:

- Security Agreement
- UCC-1
- Schedules
- Trust resolutions

All reflect **identical naming conventions**.

✓ This demonstrates proper attachment and perfection.

Method 3 — Confirm Collateral Description Meets §9-108 Standard

Checklist:

- Reasonably identifiable
- Commercial category-based
- Supported by agreement
- No illegitimate language

✓ Courts will consider it enforceable.

Method 4 — Demonstrate Attachment Occurred

You show:

- Value was given
- Debtor had rights in collateral
- Security agreement was signed

✓ Without attachment, perfection is impossible.

Method 5 — Document Internal Recordkeeping

Your administrative record should contain:

- Filing receipt
- Dated security agreement
- Ledger entries
- Trust resolutions

- Schedules

This proves:

✓ A real transaction exists
✓ Filing supports real rights

Method 6 — Maintain "Control" or "Possession" When Required

Some collateral requires control instead of filing:

- Deposit accounts
- Investment accounts

✓ Showing control = demonstrating effectiveness.

Method 7 — Show Continuation Was Filed On Time (If Needed)

If the filing continues beyond five years:

- File a continuation (UCC-3)
- Between months 48 and 60

✓ A lapse destroys priority.

XI. "Effectiveness Demonstration Package" (For Workbook Use)

Every filer should assemble:

1. **Security Agreement**
2. **UCC-1 filing receipt**
3. **Certified UCC-11 search**
4. **Schedules A, B, C**
5. **Trust or corporate resolutions authorizing filing**
6. **Internal ledger entry**
7. **Continuation calendar reminder**

This packet **proves**:

CHAPTER 7

Common Reasons UCC-1 Filings Are Ineffective

✓ Attachment
✓ Perfection
✓ Priority
✓ Continuity

Courts LOVE this.

XII. Chapter Summary

The reader now understands:

✓ Why filings fail
✓ How to avoid failure
✓ How to ensure searchability
✓ How to properly document attachment
✓ How to demonstrate effectiveness
✓ How to validate a filing post-submission
✓ How to preserve priority over time

This chapter is the bridge between **drafting** and **defending** a filing.

CHAPTER 8

What Is a UCC-3 Amendment?

Illustrated Edition — Amendments, Continuations, Terminations, and Assignments

---

I. Introduction — The UCC-3 Is the Lifeline of a Filing

A UCC-1 is not a "one and done" filing.

Over time, you may need to:

- Continue it
- Assign it
- Modify it
- Change parties
- Add collateral
- Correct errors
- Terminate it (when appropriate)

All of this is done using **UCC-3 Amendments**.

Below is your introductory visual.

CHAPTER 8

What Is a UCC-3 Amendment?

[redacted]

UCC FINANCING STATEMENT AMENDMENT

FOLLOW INSTRUCTIONS

A. NAME & PHONE OF CONTACT AT FILER (optional)

B. E-MAIL CONTACT AT FILER (optional)

C. SEND ACKNOWLEDGMENT TO: (Name and Address)

Print Reset

THE ABOVE SPACE IS FOR FILING OFFICE USE ONLY

1a. INITIAL FINANCING STATEMENT FILE NUMBER

1b. ☐ This FINANCING STATEMENT AMENDMENT is to be filed [for record] (or recorded) in the REAL ESTATE RECORDS
Filer: attach Amendment Addendum (Form UCC3Ad) and provide Debtor's name in item 13

2. ☐ TERMINATION: Effectiveness of the Financing Statement identified above is terminated with respect to the security interest(s) of Secured Party authorizing this Termination Statement

3. ☐ ASSIGNMENT (full or partial): Provide name of Assignee in item 7a or 7b, and address of Assignee in item 7c and name of Assignor in item 9
For partial assignment, complete items 7 and 9 and also indicate affected collateral in item 8

4. ☐ CONTINUATION: Effectiveness of the Financing Statement identified above with respect to the security interest(s) of Secured Party authorizing this Continuation Statement is continued for the additional period provided by applicable law

5. ☐ PARTY INFORMATION CHANGE:

Check one of these two boxes:
This Change affects ☐ Debtor or ☐ Secured Party of record

AND Check one of these three boxes to:
☐ CHANGE name and/or address: Complete item 6a or 6b; and item 7a or 7b and item 7c
☐ ADD name: Complete item 7a or 7b, and item 7c
☐ DELETE name: Give record name to be deleted in item 6a or 6b

6. CURRENT RECORD INFORMATION: Complete for Party Information Change - provide only one name (6a or 6b)

6a. ORGANIZATION'S NAME

OR

6b. INDIVIDUAL'S SURNAME	FIRST PERSONAL NAME	ADDITIONAL NAME(S)/INITIAL(S)	SUFFIX

7. CHANGED OR ADDED INFORMATION: Complete for Assignment or Party Information Change - provide only one name (7a or 7b) (use exact, full name; do not omit, modify, or abbreviate any part of the Debtor's name)

7a. ORGANIZATION'S NAME

OR

7b. INDIVIDUAL'S SURNAME

INDIVIDUAL'S FIRST PERSONAL NAME

INDIVIDUAL'S ADDITIONAL NAME(S)/INITIAL(S) | SUFFIX

7c. MAILING ADDRESS	CITY	STATE	POSTAL CODE	COUNTRY

8. ☐ COLLATERAL CHANGE: Also check one of these four boxes: ☐ ADD collateral ☐ DELETE collateral ☐ RESTATE covered collateral ☐ ASSIGN collateral

Indicate collateral:

9. NAME OF SECURED PARTY OF RECORD AUTHORIZING THIS AMENDMENT: Provide only one name (9a or 9b) (name of Assignor, if this is an Assignment)
If this is an Amendment authorized by a DEBTOR, check here ☐ and provide name of authorizing Debtor

9a. ORGANIZATION'S NAME

OR

9b. INDIVIDUAL'S SURNAME	FIRST PERSONAL NAME	ADDITIONAL NAME(S)/INITIAL(S)	SUFFIX

10. OPTIONAL FILER REFERENCE DATA:

International Association of Commercial Administrators (IACA)

FILING OFFICE COPY — UCC FINANCING STATEMENT AMENDMENT (Form UCC3) (Rev. 04/20/11)

CHAPTER 8

What Is a UCC-3 Amendment?

II. The Five Functions of a UCC-3 Amendment

A UCC-3 can legally perform the following:

1. **Amend**
2. **Continue**
3. **Assign**
4. **Terminate**
5. **Correct** (Non-standard but permitted depending on state)

Let's explore each in full.

III. UCC-3 Function #1 — AMEND (Modify Party Info or Collateral)

You use an amendment when:

- Debtor name changes
- Secured party name changes
- Collateral needs modification
- You need to add collateral
- You need to delete collateral

An amendment does **not**:

- Change the original filing date
- Reset priority
- Replace the UCC-1

Visual:

A. Example: Adding Collateral

Original collateral:

"Equipment and inventory."

Amended collateral:

"Equipment, inventory, accounts, general intangibles, and proceeds."

CHAPTER 8

What Is a UCC-3 Amendment?

✓ Priority for *new collateral* dates from amendment
✓ Priority for *old collateral* stays with original UCC-1

B. Example: Correcting Trust Name

Original (incorrect):

"Rodney Carroll ElAli Trust"

Correct:

"Rodney Cortez Carroll-El Ali Living Trust"

✓ Amendment fixes indexing
✓ Filing becomes discoverable
✓ You preserve priority

IV. UCC-3 Function #2 — CONTINUE (Extend the Filing Beyond 5 Years)

A UCC-1 expires after **five years** unless continued.

The continuation:

- Must be filed *within the 6-month window*
- Must be filed by the secured party
- Extends filing another 5 years
- Does **not** alter priority

A. Continuation Window Rule

You can only file a continuation:

- Between **month 48 and month 60** after original filing

Filed too early → Rejected
Filed too late → Filing lapses

If it lapses:

- You lose all priority
- The filing cannot be revived
- You must file a new UCC-1 with a **new** priority date

CHAPTER 8

What Is a UCC-3 Amendment?

B. Example Using Your Entities

Original UCC-1:
Filed January 1, 2025
Expires January 1, 2030

Continuation window:
July 1, 2029 – January 1, 2030

If RE 234 270 824 US Holdings forgets to continue the filing — the trust loses priority.

V. UCC-3 Function #3 — ASSIGN (Transfer Secured Party Rights)

Assignments are powerful.
They allow you to:

- Move secured interests between trusts
- Transfer interests to new LLCs
- Reorganize internal structures
- Sell secured interests to third parties

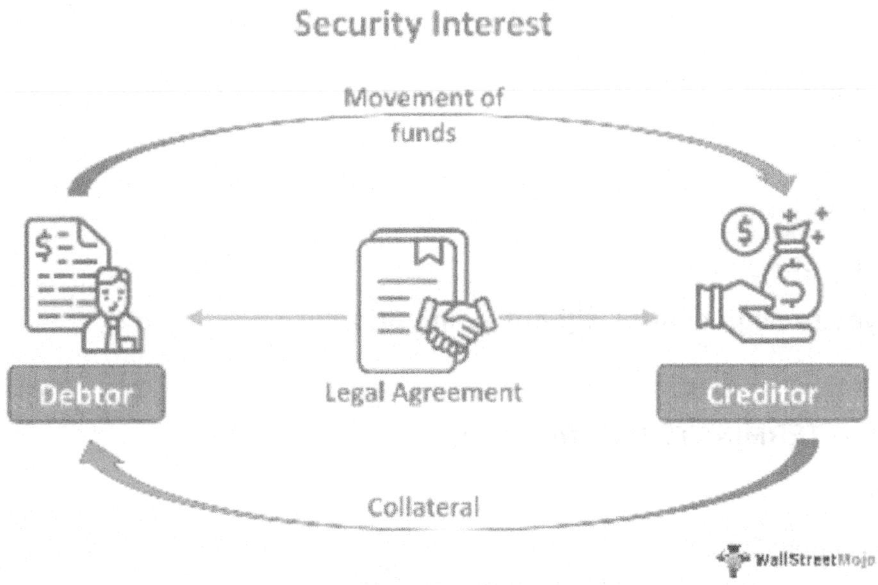

A. Full Assignment

The entire secured interest transfers to the new secured party.

CHAPTER 8

What Is a UCC-3 Amendment?

Example:
Secured Party changes from:
Rodney Cortez Carroll-El Ali Living Trust

To:
RE 234 270 824 US Holdings

✓ New secured party now holds full rights
✓ Priority date stays the same

B. Partial Assignment

Only part of the collateral is assigned.

Example:

Assign "accounts and payment intangibles" to Trust A
Assign "equipment" to Trust B

✓ Allowed under Article 9
✓ Each secured party must be listed

C. Why Assignments Matter in Your Structure

You often transition:

- From personal → trust
- Trust → holding trust
- Holding trust → LLC
- LLC → operating trust

Assignments are **how you re-align control without losing priority**.

VI. UCC-3 Function #4 — TERMINATE (End the Filing)

A termination is serious.

Only the **secured party** should file one —
unless the debtor has evidence the obligation has been satisfied.

A termination:

- Removes the filing from the active index

CHAPTER 8

What Is a UCC-3 Amendment?

- Ends perfection
- Ends priority
- Ends the security interest

A. Appropriate Reasons to Terminate

- Debt is paid in full
- Collateral returned
- Contract ends
- Parties close the relationship

B. NEVER Terminate If…

- You still want priority
- You may refinance the loan
- You may restructure the collateral
- You plan to assign the interest

Terminating relinquishes all power.

C. Preventing Fraudulent Terminations

Debtors sometimes attempt to wipe out filings by filing unauthorized terminations.

Preventive steps:

✓ Keep certified records
✓ Demonstrate attachment
✓ Demonstrate effectiveness (Chapter 7 methods)
✓ Refile immediately with documentation

Some states allow fraud-blocking notices.

VII. UCC-3 Function #5 — CORRECT (Non-Standard but Important)

A correction is used when:

- A typo exists
- Address is wrong

CHAPTER 8

What Is a UCC-3 Amendment?

- Trust name changed
- Entity converted (LLC → Corp.)
- Party was mis listed

Some states treat corrections as amendments.
Others provide a specific checkbox.

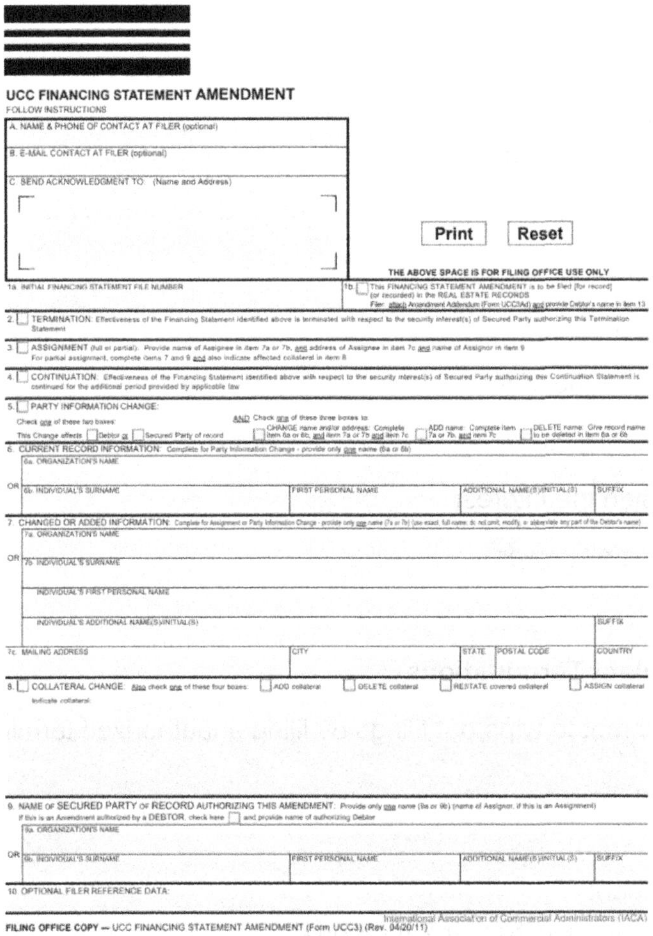

UCC FINANCING STATEMENT AMENDMENT

FOLLOW INSTRUCTIONS

A. NAME & PHONE OF CONTACT AT FILER (optional)

B. E-MAIL CONTACT AT FILER (optional)

C. SEND ACKNOWLEDGMENT TO: (Name and Address)

Print Reset

THE ABOVE SPACE IS FOR FILING OFFICE USE ONLY

1a. INITIAL FINANCING STATEMENT FILE NUMBER

1b. ☐ This FINANCING STATEMENT AMENDMENT is to be filed [for record] (or recorded) in the REAL ESTATE RECORDS
Filer: attach Amendment Addendum (Form UCC3Ad) and provide Debtor's name in item 13

2. ☐ TERMINATION: Effectiveness of the Financing Statement identified above is terminated with respect to the security interest(s) of Secured Party authorizing this Termination Statement

3. ☐ ASSIGNMENT (full or partial): Provide name of Assignee in item 7a or 7b, and address of Assignee in item 7c and name of Assignor in item 9
For partial assignment, complete items 7 and 9 and also indicate affected collateral in item 8

4. ☐ CONTINUATION: Effectiveness of the Financing Statement identified above with respect to the security interest(s) of Secured Party authorizing this Continuation Statement is continued for the additional period provided by applicable law

5. ☐ PARTY INFORMATION CHANGE:
Check one of these two boxes:
This Change affects ☐ Debtor or ☐ Secured Party of record
AND Check one of these three boxes to:
☐ CHANGE name and/or address: Complete item 6a or 6b, and item 7a or 7b and item 7c
☐ ADD name: Complete item 7a or 7b, and item 7c
☐ DELETE name: Give record name to be deleted in item 6a or 6b

6. CURRENT RECORD INFORMATION: Complete for Party Information Change - provide only one name (6a or 6b)
6a. ORGANIZATION'S NAME
OR 6b. INDIVIDUAL'S SURNAME | FIRST PERSONAL NAME | ADDITIONAL NAME(S)/INITIAL(S) | SUFFIX

7. CHANGED OR ADDED INFORMATION: Complete for Assignment or Party Information Change - provide only one name (7a or 7b) (use exact, full name; do not omit, modify, or abbreviate any part of the Debtor's name)
7a. ORGANIZATION'S NAME
OR 7b. INDIVIDUAL'S SURNAME
INDIVIDUAL'S FIRST PERSONAL NAME
INDIVIDUAL'S ADDITIONAL NAME(S)/INITIAL(S) | SUFFIX
7c. MAILING ADDRESS | CITY | STATE | POSTAL CODE | COUNTRY

8. ☐ COLLATERAL CHANGE: Also check one of these four boxes: ☐ ADD collateral ☐ DELETE collateral ☐ RESTATE covered collateral ☐ ASSIGN collateral
Indicate collateral:

9. NAME OF SECURED PARTY OF RECORD AUTHORIZING THIS AMENDMENT: Provide only one name (9a or 9b) (name of Assignor, if this is an Assignment)
If this is an Amendment authorized by a DEBTOR, check here ☐ and provide name of authorizing Debtor
9a. ORGANIZATION'S NAME
OR 9b. INDIVIDUAL'S SURNAME | FIRST PERSONAL NAME | ADDITIONAL NAME(S)/INITIAL(S) | SUFFIX

10. OPTIONAL FILER REFERENCE DATA:

FILING OFFICE COPY — UCC FINANCING STATEMENT AMENDMENT (Form UCC3) (Rev. 04/20/11)

International Association of Commercial Administrators (IACA)

VIII. The UCC-3 Does NOT Change the Original Priority Date

Even after:

- Amendments
- Assignments
- Debtor changes

- Secured party changes
- Collateral changes

The original date stands.
Unless:

- The filing lapses
- You terminate
- You file new collateral (priority applies only to new collateral)

IX. Complete Filing Flow: UCC-1 → UCC-3 Lifecycle

Time to tie the entire lifecycle visually.

X. Real-World Trust-Based Amendment Examples

These examples teach you exactly how to apply amendments.

Example 1 — Adding New Collateral Later

Original UCC-1 collateral:

"Equipment and inventory."

After business expansion:

UCC-3 amendment adds:

"Accounts, payment intangibles, general intangibles, and proceeds thereof."

✓ Old collateral keeps original priority
✓ New collateral priority begins on amendment date

Example 2 — Assigning Filing to the Holding Trust

Original Secured Party:

Rodney Cortez Carroll-El Ali Living Trust

UCC-3 Assignment → New Secured Party:

RE 234 270 824 US Holdings

CHAPTER 8

What Is a UCC-3 Amendment?

✓ Maintains priority
✓ Establishes clean administrative hierarchy
✓ Creates structured estate control

Example 3 — Continuing Before Expiration

You set automated reminders:

- Month 48
- Month 54
- Month 59

UCC-3 Continuation filed during month 55:

✓ Filing now extended to 2035
✓ No lapse
✓ Priority preserved

Example 4 — Correcting the Debtor Name

If Babylon Industries LLC was originally filed as:

"Babylon Industry LLC"

UCC-3 Correction fixes it, preserving enforceability.

XI. Chapter Summary

Readers now understand:

✓ What each UCC-3 function does
✓ How to amend collateral
✓ How to continue a filing
✓ How to assign secured interests between trusts
✓ How to terminate safely
✓ How to correct errors
✓ Why priority is preserved
✓ How UCC-3 filings fit into the full lifecycle

This chapter is essential for Chapter 9 (Continuations) and Chapter 10 (Assignments).

CHAPTER 8

What Is a UCC-3 Amendment?

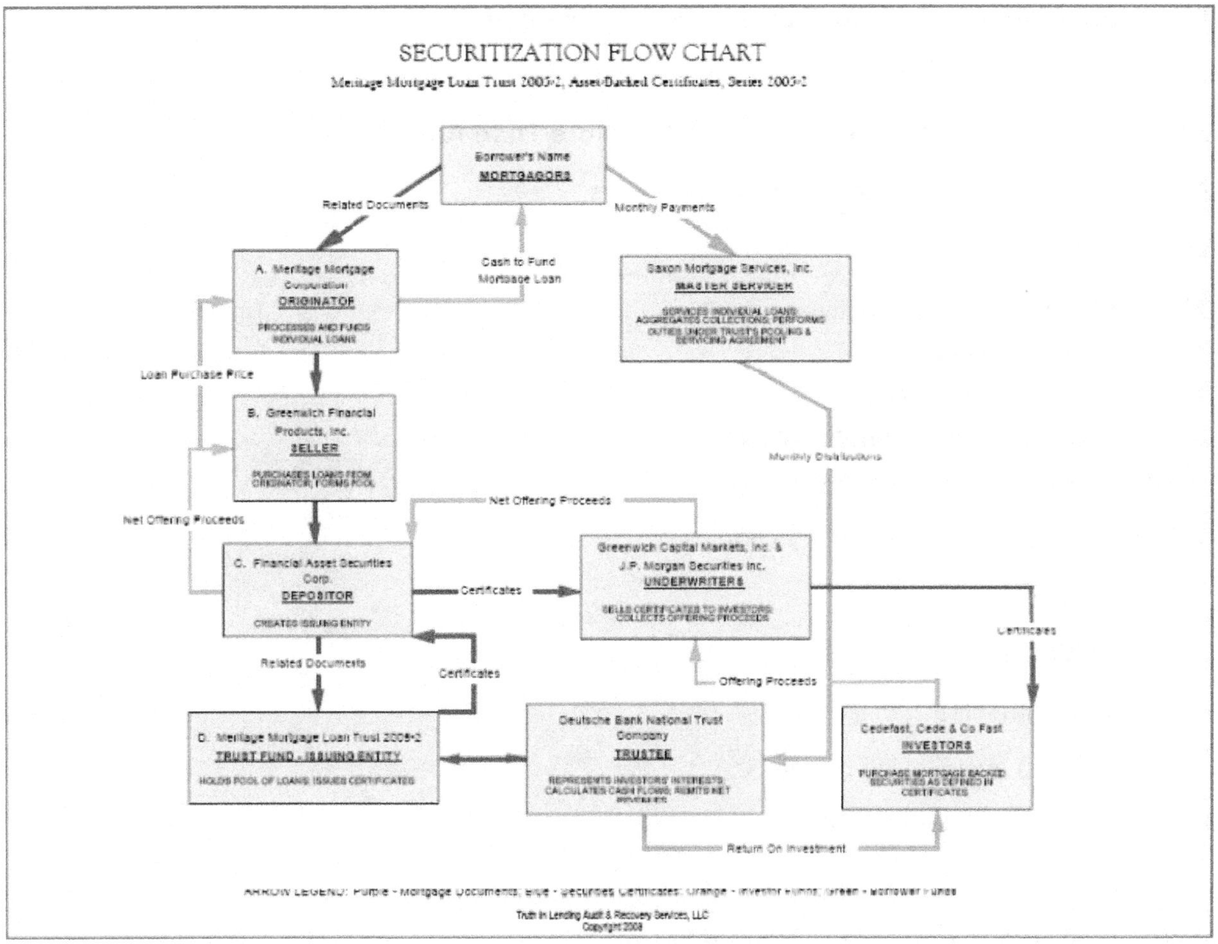

CHAPTER 9

Continuations (The 5-Year Rule)

Illustrated Edition — How to Preserve Priority Forever

I. Introduction — Why Continuations Matter More Than Amendments

A UCC-1 automatically lapses after **five (5) years**.

When it lapses:

❌ The filing becomes ineffective
❌ All perfection is lost
❌ Priority disappears instantly
❌ A new UCC-1 restarts priority at zero
❌ Other creditors can bypass you

This chapter teaches the exact mechanics of:

- WHEN to file
- HOW to file
- WHO must file
- HOW to avoid losing priority

Here is your introductory visual.

II. What a Continuation Is (and What It Is Not)

A **continuation** is a UCC-3 amendment that:

✓ Extends the UCC-1 for another 5 years
✓ Keeps the ORIGINAL priority date
✓ Must be filed by the secured party
✓ Must be filed during a specific 6-month window

A continuation does *not*:

✗ Modify collateral
✗ Replace the UCC-1
✗ Change debtor or secured party
✗ Increase or reduce rights

It simply **keeps your lien alive**.

CHAPTER 9

Continuations (The 5-Year Rule)

III. The Continuation Window (The Most Important Rule in Chapter 9)

A continuation may be filed **ONLY**:

✓ **Between month 48 and month 60**

before the 5-year expiration.

This is known as the **Continuation Window**.

Filing:

- Too early → INVALID
- Too late → INVALID
- After expiration → TOO LATE

IV. What Happens If You Miss the Window (Critical)

If the continuation is NOT filed within the window:

The filing lapses.

A lapse causes:

✗ Immediate loss of perfection
✗ Loss of priority
✗ All new creditors jump ahead
✗ The filing cannot be revived
✗ A new UCC-1 must be filed
✗ Priority restarts from zero

This is one of the fastest ways creditors lose secured rights.

V. Filing the Continuation — Step-by-Step

Step 1 — Locate the UCC-1 Filing Number

Needed to reference the original filing.

Step 2 — Prepare the UCC-3

Select **CONTINUATION** as the amendment type.

Step 3 — File in the Same Jurisdiction

Continuation must be filed in the state where the UCC-1 is indexed.

CHAPTER 9

Continuations (The 5-Year Rule)

Step 4 — Pay the Fee

Usually $10–$20.

Step 5 — Confirm Acceptance

SOS issues acknowledgement with the new expiration date.

Step 6 — Store the Filing Receipt

Place in your trust or business administrative record.

Below is the visual.

VI. Who Can File a Continuation?

✓ Only the secured party

or
✓ An authorized representative of the secured party.

A debtor cannot file a continuation.

A debtor can only file a **termination**
— and only when the obligation has been satisfied.

This distinction prevents manipulation.

VII. Priority Rules for Continuations

One of the biggest benefits of a continuation is:

✓ Priority date DOES NOT change.

This is critical for:

- Secured party protection
- Bankruptcy priority
- Inter-creditor disputes
- Trust-based long-term strategy

Below is the priority visual.

CHAPTER 9

Continuations (The 5-Year Rule)

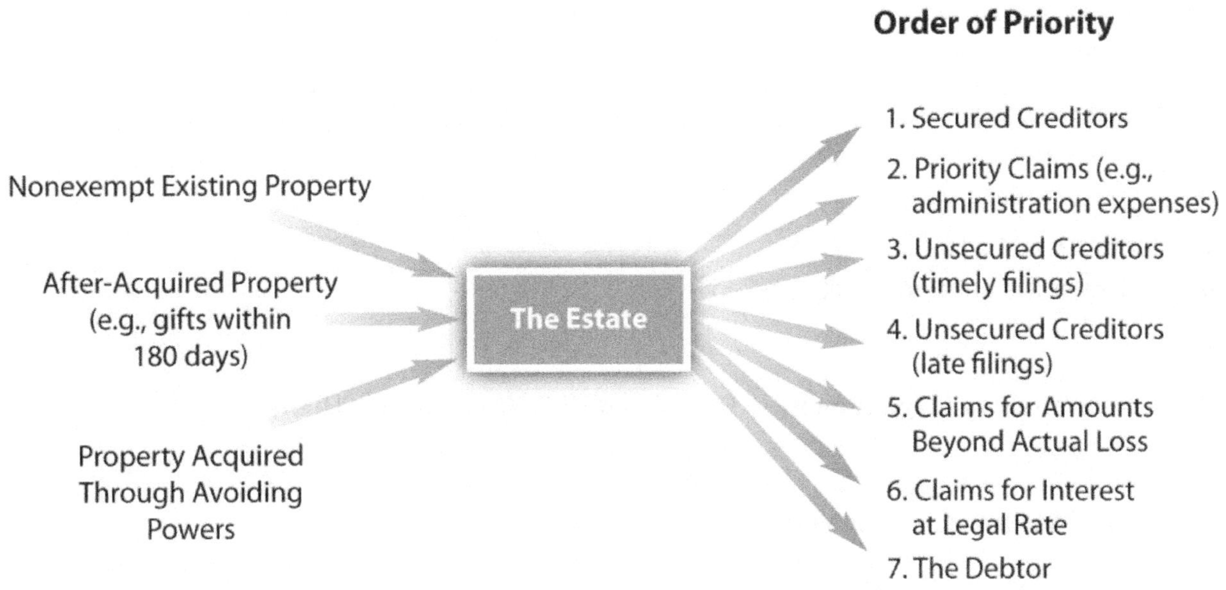

VIII. Example Timelines (Using Your Entities)

Example 1 — Trust Securing Business Collateral

Secured Party:
RE 234 270 824 US Holdings

Debtor:
Babylon Industries LLC

UCC-1 Filed: March 1, 2025
Expires: March 1, 2030

Continuation window:
September 1, 2029 → March 1, 2030

If continued:

✓ Original priority date: 2025
✓ Next expiration: 2035

Example 2 — Living Trust Securing Beneficiary Loan

Secured Party:
Rodney Cortez Carroll-El Ali Living Trust

Debtor:
Individual beneficiary

CHAPTER 9

Continuations (The 5-Year Rule)

Filed: July 7, 2024
Expires: July 7, 2029

Continuation window:
January 7, 2029 → July 7, 2029

Filing a continuation preserves:
✓ Priority against all future lenders
✓ Claim over the collateral until satisfied

IX. Continuation vs. Amendment — Readers MUST Not Confuse Them

An amendment:

- Modifies parties or collateral
- Does NOT extend expiration

A continuation:

- Extends expiration
- Does NOT modify parties or collateral

Common mistake:

People think filing *an amendment* extends time.
It does **not**.

X. Continuation Best Practices (Professional-Grade Strategy)

✓ 1. Set a digital reminder for month 48

Never let the window sneak up.

✓ 2. Log continuation date in trust minute books

Courts love documentary consistency.

✓ 3. Keep all continuation receipts

To demonstrate uninterrupted perfection.

✓ 4. Use consistent email and SOS accounts

Avoid login confusion across states.

✓ 5. Review collateral at continuation time

CHAPTER 9

Continuations (The 5-Year Rule)

Amend collateral *before* continuing if needed.

✓ 6. Check debtor name again

If debtor changed name, amend before or at continuation.

✓ 7. Run a UCC-11 Search Before Continuing

This is extremely powerful for demonstrating effectiveness.

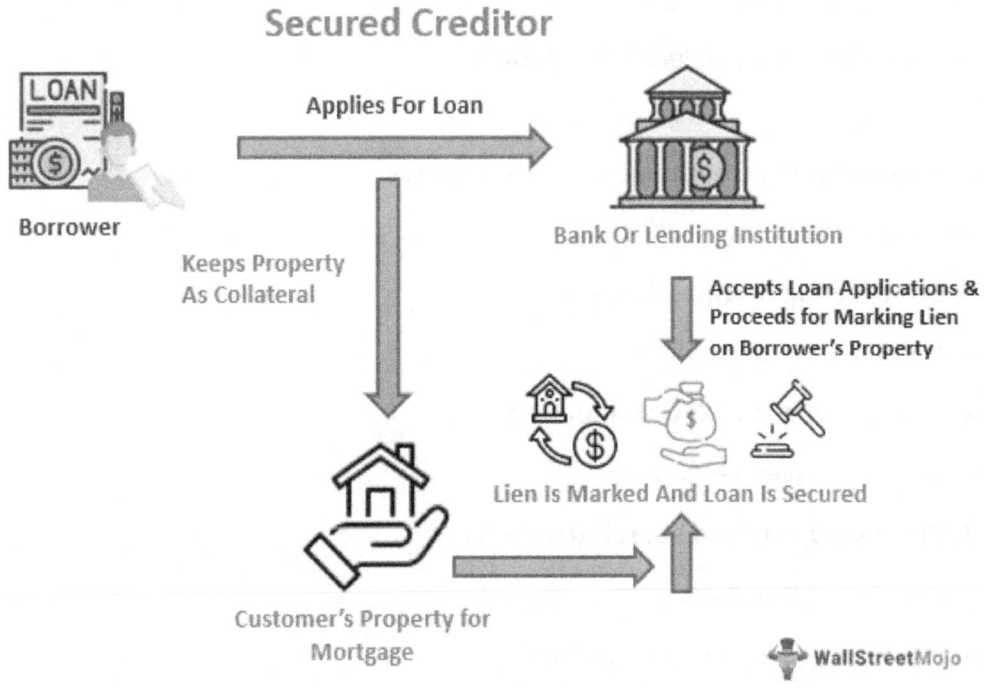

XI. Preventing Lapse — The "No-Lapse System"

Teach your readers to maintain perfection for decades.

The 3-Level Protection Model:

Level 1 — Calendar Automation

Set automatic reminders annually and in month 48.

Level 2 — Trust or Business Filing Log

Maintain a table listing:

- Filing number

- Date filed
- Date expiring
- Date continuation due

Level 3 — Yearly Verification

Every 12 months:

- Run a debtor search
- Verify filing is still active
- Confirm no fraudulent termination

XII. Demonstrating Continuation Effectiveness

To show a continuation is effective:

✓ 1. Produce the original UCC-1

Shows the original priority date.

✓ 2. Produce the UCC-3 Continuation

Shows uninterrupted perfection.

✓ 3. Produce a certified search (UCC-11)

Shows both filings appear.

✓ 4. Produce the security agreement

Shows attachment remains valid.

✓ 5. Produce trust resolutions (if trust-based)

Shows internal authority to maintain lien.

This creates a **perfect evidence chain**.

XIII. Chapter Summary

Readers now understand:

✓ What a continuation is
✓ How it preserves priority
✓ Why timing is critical

CHAPTER 9

Continuations (The 5-Year Rule)

✓ How to file correctly
✓ How to prevent lapses
✓ How amendments differ from continuations
✓ How to demonstrate legal effectiveness
✓ How trust entities maintain long-term perfection

This chapter prepares the reader for **Chapter 10 — Assignments**, which will explain transferring secured interests cleanly and legally between entities.

CHAPTER 10

Assignments, Transfers, and Reorganization Filings

Illustrated Edition — How to Transfer Secured Interests Without Losing Priority

---

I. Introduction — Why Assignments Are Used in Real-World Strategies

Assignments allow secured parties to:

- Move interests between entities
- Reorganize their estate structure
- Consolidate secured interests
- Transfer rights to a holding trust
- Distribute collateral interests among trusts
- Sell a secured interest commercially
- Prevent loss of priority during restructuring

Assignments are the backbone of:

- Corporate reorganizations
- Trust administration
- Holding company strategies
- Multi-tier asset protection
- Inter-creditor relationships

II. What Is a UCC Assignment?

A UCC assignment is a UCC-3 Amendment that transfers **some or all** of the secured party's rights to another party.

Assignments can be:

✓ FULL

All rights under the UCC-1 transfer to the new secured party.

✓ PARTIAL

Only certain rights or collateral categories transfer.

Assignments **do NOT** change:

- Debtor name
- Collateral (unless modified)
- The original priority date

This is why assignments are powerful.

III. Two Types of Assignments (Full vs. Partial)

Below is the visual breakdown.

A. Full Assignment — "Transfer EVERYTHING"

Example:

Original Secured Party:
Rodney Cortez Carroll-El Ali Living Trust

New Secured Party:
RE 234 270 824 US Holdings

After assignment:

✓ All rights transfer
✓ All claims transfer
✓ All remedies transfer
✓ Original priority date remains

This is the cleanest method of reorganizing secured interests.

B. Partial Assignment — "Transfer SOME Rights"

Example:

Transfer rights in **accounts and payment intangibles**
But retain rights in **equipment and inventory**

Partial assignments are used for:

- Joint secured interests
- Multi-trust asset protection
- Shared creditor rights

CHAPTER 10

Assignments, Transfers, and Reorganization Filings

- Private lending syndicates

Both structures are valid under Article 9.

IV. Why Use Assignments? (Strategic Reasons)

Assignments are used when:

✓ Trust structure evolves

✓ A holding trust takes over administration

✓ A new LLC becomes the operating entity

✓ Control must be centralized

✓ Ownership interests shift

✓ A secured interest is sold or transferred

✓ Assets move between related entities

Trust ecosystems like yours often evolve in stages:

1. Individual → Living Trust
2. Living Trust → Holding Trust
3. Holding Trust → LLC
4. LLC → Project Trust

Assignments make this legally seamless.

V. How to File an Assignment (Step-by-Step)

Step 1 — Locate the Original Filing Number

Needed for the UCC-3.

Step 2 — Prepare the UCC-3

Select **ASSIGNMENT** as the amendment type.

Step 3 — List the "Assignor" and "Assignee"

CHAPTER 10

Assignments, Transfers, and Reorganization Filings

Assignor = Current secured party
Assignee = New secured party

Step 4 — Indicate Full or Partial Assignment

If partial, specify which collateral.

Step 5 — File in the Same Jurisdiction

Always file where the UCC-1 is indexed.

Step 6 — Receive Filing Acknowledgement

Store in trust/LLC administrative record.

VII. Example Assignment Filings Using YOUR Structure

These are real-world examples your readers can learn from.

Example 1 — Living Trust → Holding Trust (Full Assignment)

Original Secured Party:
Rodney Cortez Carroll-El Ali Living Trust

New Secured Party:
RE 234 270 824 US Holdings

✓ Priority preserved
✓ Holding trust now controls secured rights
✓ Clean administrative structure

Example 2 — Holding Trust → LLC (Partial Assignment)

Assign:

✓ "Accounts, payment intangibles, general intangibles"

Retain:

✓ "Equipment and inventory"

Purpose:

- LLC receives revenue stream rights

CHAPTER 10

Assignments, Transfers, and Reorganization Filings

- Holding trust retains hard-asset control

Example 3 — LLC → Trust (Reorganization)

If Babylon Industries LLC restructures:

Assignor: Babylon Industries LLC
Assignee: Rodney Cortez Carroll-El Ali Living Trust

Reason:

- Trust takes over financing
- Business shifts into trust jurisdiction

Example 4 — Multi-Trust Shared Secured Interest

Trust A and Trust B share priority for different collateral types.

This is advanced structuring — and completely lawful.

VIII. Priority Rules for Assignments

Article 9 is VERY clear:

✓ Assignments DO NOT change the priority date.

Priority remains:

- The original UCC-1 filing date
- Even if the secured party changes
- Even if collateral is modified
- Even if ownership restructures

This is the single greatest benefit of using assignments.

IX. Special Case — Assigning Collateral After Amendments

If collateral was amended:

- Old collateral retains original priority
- New collateral has priority from amendment date

CHAPTER 10

Assignments, Transfers, and Reorganization Filings

- Assignment does not alter either timeline

This is important for:

- Growing businesses
- Trust expansions
- Adding new assets

X. Demonstrating Assignment Effectiveness (Court-Safe Method)

To prove an assignment is effective, create a **four-document chain**:

1. Original UCC-1 Filing

Shows original priority.

2. Security Agreement(s)

Attach all relevant agreements.

3. UCC-3 Assignment Filing

Shows transfer of secured rights.

4. Certified UCC-11 Search

Shows BOTH filings appear in the public record.

This documentation chain is recognized in every jurisdiction.

Below is the visual.

Image: "Proof Package" for Demonstrating Assignment Effectiveness

CHAPTER 10

Assignments, Transfers, and Reorganization Filings

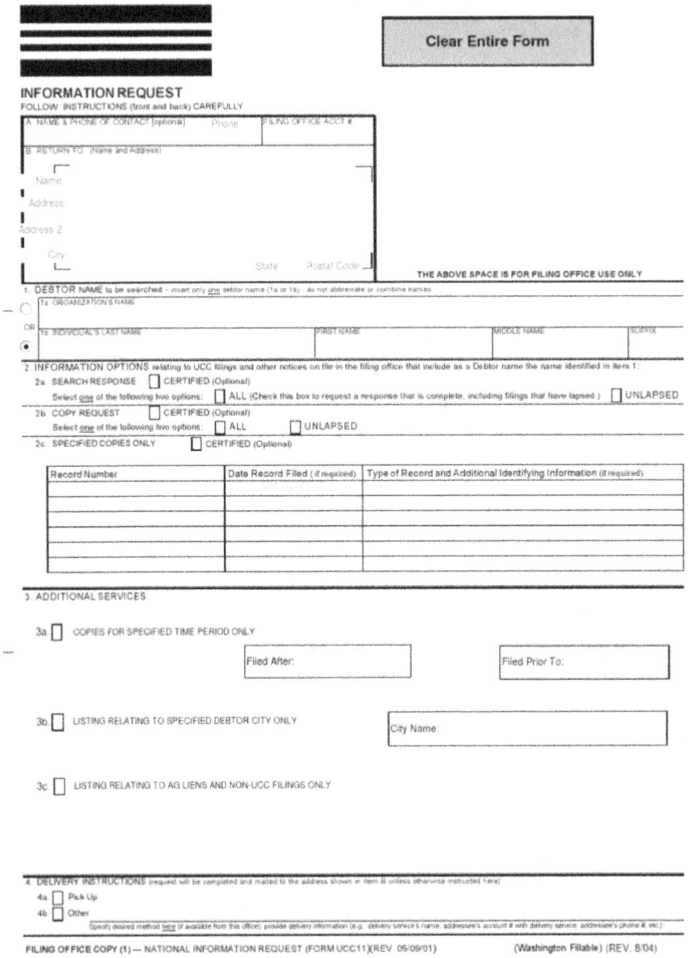

Clear Entire Form

INFORMATION REQUEST

FOLLOW INSTRUCTIONS (front and back) CAREFULLY

A. NAME & PHONE OF CONTACT [optional] Phone | FILING OFFICE ACCT #

B. RETURN TO: (Name and Address)

Name

Address

Address 2

City State Postal Code

THE ABOVE SPACE IS FOR FILING OFFICE USE ONLY

1. DEBTOR NAME to be searched - insert only one debtor name (1a or 1b) - do not abbreviate or combine names

1a. ORGANIZATION'S NAME

OR

1b. INDIVIDUAL'S LAST NAME | FIRST NAME | MIDDLE NAME | SUFFIX

2. INFORMATION OPTIONS relating to UCC filings and other notices on file in the filing office that include as a Debtor name the name identified in item 1:

2a. SEARCH RESPONSE ☐ CERTIFIED (Optional)

Select one of the following two options: ☐ ALL (Check this box to request a response that is complete, including filings that have lapsed.) ☐ UNLAPSED

2b. COPY REQUEST ☐ CERTIFIED (Optional)

Select one of the following two options: ☐ ALL ☐ UNLAPSED

2c. SPECIFIED COPIES ONLY ☐ CERTIFIED (Optional)

Record Number	Date Record Filed (if required)	Type of Record and Additional Identifying Information (if required)

3. ADDITIONAL SERVICES:

3a. ☐ COPIES FOR SPECIFIED TIME PERIOD ONLY

Filed After: | Filed Prior To:

3b. ☐ LISTING RELATING TO SPECIFIED DEBTOR CITY ONLY

City Name:

3c. ☐ LISTING RELATING TO AG LIENS AND NON-UCC FILINGS ONLY

4. DELIVERY INSTRUCTIONS (request will be completed and mailed to the address shown in item B unless otherwise instructed here)

4a. ☐ Pick Up

4b. ☐ Other

Specify desired method here (if available from this office): provide delivery information (e.g., delivery service's name, addressee's account # with delivery service, addressee's phone #, etc.)

FILING OFFICE COPY (1) — NATIONAL INFORMATION REQUEST (FORM UCC11)(REV. 05/09/01) (Washington Fillable) (REV. 8/04)

Instructions for National Information Request (Form UCC11)

XI. How Assignments Strengthen a Trust Ecosystem

Assignments allow you to:

✓ Move secured rights without rewriting contracts

✓ Centralize power in a holding trust

✓ Transfer enforcement powers legally

✓ Protect estates during restructuring

✓ Maintain clean administrative lineage

✓ Ensure your UCC system evolves with you

This is how generational trust systems maintain continuity.

CHAPTER 10

Assignments, Transfers, and Reorganization Filings

XII. Chapter Summary

Your reader now understands:

✓ What assignments are
✓ Why assignments matter
✓ How to file them properly
✓ Full vs partial assignments
✓ Trust → trust transfers
✓ LLC → trust transfers
✓ How priority is preserved
✓ How to demonstrate assignment effectiveness
✓ How assignments support reorganizations

This chapter makes your guidebook **operational**, not just educational.

CHAPTER 11

Terminations, Corrections, and Protective Filings

Illustrated Edition — Protecting Secured Interests & Preventing Administrative Abuse

---

I. Introduction — The Most Sensitive Filings in the UCC System

Amendments and continuations are routine.
Assignments are strategic.

But **terminations and corrections** are *surgical* —
a single wrong move can:

❌ Destroy perfection
❌ Eliminate priority
❌ Remove enforcement rights
❌ Expose assets
❌ Break the administrative chain
❌ Invite creditor challenges

On the positive side:

✓ Proper terminations officially release a lien
✓ Corrective filings preserve integrity
✓ Protective filings prevent attacks
✓ Internal records can shield secured rights

Here is your introductory visual.

II. Section One — TERMINATIONS (UCC-3 Terminations)

Used to END a security interest — permanently.

A termination filing:

- Removes the UCC-1 from the active index
- Ends perfection
- Ends priority
- Ends the secured party's claim
- Returns collateral to unencumbered status

Terminations must be used with precision.

III. When Should a Termination Be Filed?

CHAPTER 11

Terminations, Corrections, and Protective Filings

✓ When the debtor fully satisfies the secured obligation

Loan repaid → terminate.

✓ When the parties end the security arrangement

Contract concludes → terminate.

✓ When collateral is returned or liquidated

Security interest no longer exists → terminate.

✓ When trust administration shifts and lien is no longer needed

Reorganization complete → terminate.

IV. When SHOULD NOT a Termination Be Filed

Never terminate if:

✗ You still want priority
✗ The debt isn't fully satisfied
✗ Collateral remains encumbered
✗ You expect refinancing or restructuring
✗ You intend to reassign the secured interest
✗ You anticipate litigation or enforcement

Priority is not regained once terminated.

Priority is **killed.**

Once gone → gone forever.

V. Fraudulent or Unauthorized Terminations (VERY IMPORTANT)

How debtors try to wipe out liens — and how to stop them.

Some debtors attempt:

- Filing unauthorized terminations
- Filing false claims of satisfaction
- Filing bogus amendments
- Filing terminations pretending to be the secured party

This is a growing issue in commercial lending.

CHAPTER 11

Terminations, Corrections, and Protective Filings

A. SOS Offices DO NOT Verify Authority

They do not:

- Check the security agreement
- Check signatures
- Validate claims
- Confirm authority

They're clerical, not judicial.

This is why **protective filings** (next section) are essential.

B. What to Do If Someone Files an Unauthorized Termination

You must:

1. **Immediately refile a UCC-1** (to stop further damage)
2. **File a UCC-5 Information Statement** contesting the termination
3. **File a corrective UCC-3 amendment** (in some states)
4. **Provide evidence of attachment + original filing**
5. **Run a certified UCC-11 search** for proof of tampering

We will illustrate this later.

VI. Section Two — CORRECTIONS (Correcting Errors Without Losing Priority)

A UCC correction is used to fix:

- Typographical errors
- Name misspellings
- Wrong addresses
- Trust name updates
- Entity conversions
- Minor filing mistakes

CHAPTER 11

Terminations, Corrections, and Protective Filings

Corrections are sometimes done via UCC-3 amendment;
other states have a specific correction form.

VII. Critical Rule — Corrections Do NOT Reset Priority

Correcting a filing:

✓ Preserves original date
✓ Preserves priority
✓ Strengthens enforceability
✓ Fixes search logic issues

But corrections **cannot**:

✕ Fix a lapse
✕ Fix a fraudulent termination
✕ Fix illegal collateral
✕ Fix wrong jurisdiction
✕ Fix filings with no underlying agreement

Corrections only fix *technical defects*, not legal defects.

VIII. Section Three — PROTECTIVE FILINGS (Your Secret Weapon)

These protect against fraud, tampering, and administrative abuse.

Protective filings are used to:

✓ Notify the public of pending disputes
✓ Declare unauthorized terminations as invalid
✓ Block fraudulent filings from taking effect
✓ Document your priority claim
✓ Establish your "chain of authority"

These include:

1. **UCC-5 Information Statements**
2. **Protective Amendments**
3. **Authority Declarations**
4. **Administrative Notices**

CHAPTER 11

Terminations, Corrections, and Protective Filings

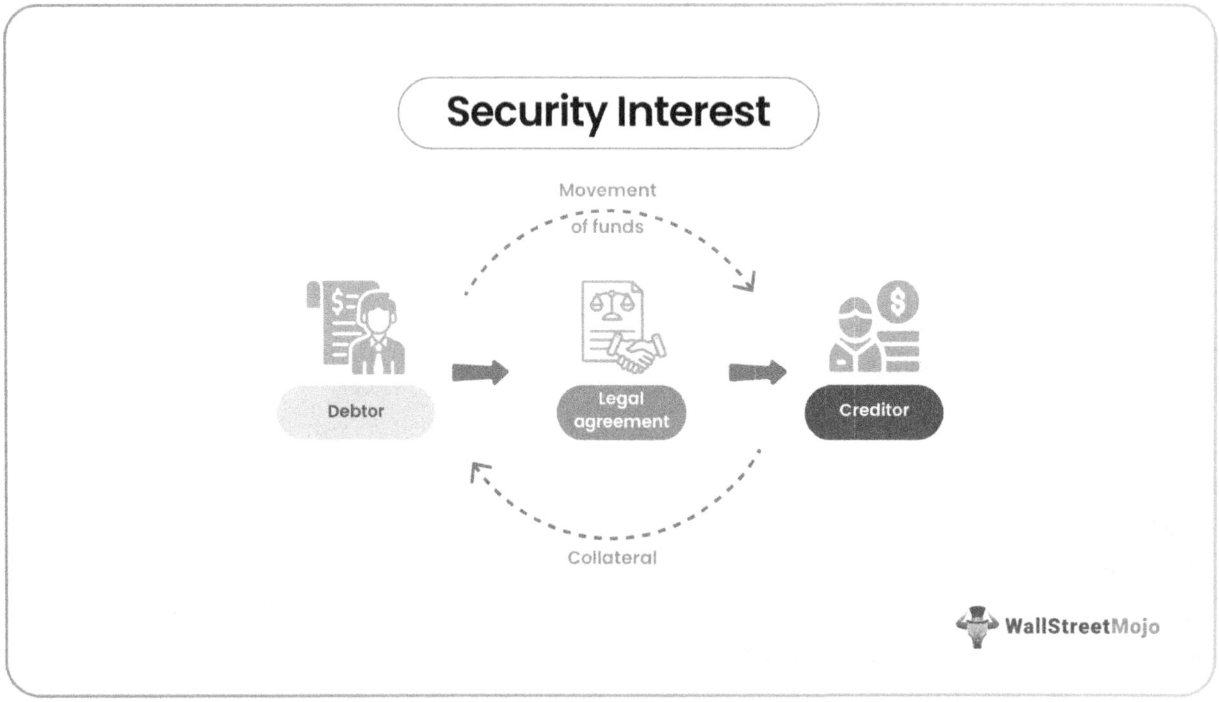

IX. UCC-5 Information Statement (Most Underused Tool)

This DOES NOT alter the filing — it protects it.

You use a UCC-5 to:

- Declare a filing fraudulent
- Declare a termination unauthorized
- Clarify your secured party rights
- Put third parties on notice
- Document your administrative position

A UCC-5:

✓ Creates a permanent record
✓ Alerts all future searchers
✓ Strengthens your legal position
✓ Provides evidence in litigation

But:

✗ It does not restore a lapsed filing
✗ It does not reverse a termination
✗ It does not change priority

It is purely a **protective shield**.

X. Real-World Example — Debtor Attempts Unauthorized Termination

Scenario

Debtor tries to terminate a lien filed by:

Secured Party:
RE 234 270 824 US Holdings

Response:

✓ File a UCC-5 contesting the termination
✓ Refile a UCC-1 with reference to original
✓ File a UCC-3 correction or reassertion
✓ Present your security agreement
✓ Run a certified search to create a legal evidence packet

This is the exact process businesses and banks use.

CHAPTER 11

Terminations, Corrections, and Protective Filings

XI. How to Demonstrate Effectiveness After a Correction or Protection Filing

To prove your corrected or protected filing is effective:

1. Produce the original UCC-1
2. Produce the correction (UCC-3 or state equivalent)
3. Produce security agreements
4. Produce a certified UCC-11 search showing both filings
5. Produce trust/LLC resolutions authorizing the correction
6. Produce internal ledger entries
7. Produce protective notices (if applicable)

This creates a chain-of-evidence Courts love.

XII. Complete Trust-Based Example

Original Structure

Secured Party: Rodney Cortez Carroll-El Ali Living Trust
Debtor: Babylon Industries LLC

Mistake in Filing

Debtor listed as "Bablyon Industries LLC" (misspelled)

Correction

UCC-3 Correction filed with proper spelling.

Protective Filing

UCC-5 filed documenting:

✓ The original agreement
✓ The error
✓ The correction
✓ Declaration of continued effectiveness

Result

✓ Priority maintained
✓ Filing preserved

✓ Search logic repaired
✓ Administrative chain intact

Perfect outcome.

XIII. Chapter Summary

Readers now understand:

✓ When to terminate properly
✓ How to avoid losing priority
✓ How to prevent unauthorized terminations
✓ How to correct a filing safely
✓ How to protect their filings
✓ How UCC-5 information statements work
✓ How to build a chain-of-evidence for enforceability
✓ How to maintain a clean, fraud-resistant administrative record

This chapter empowers your readers to guard their secured interests like professionals.

CHAPTER 12

Enforcement Basics & What a UCC Filing REALLY Does in Practice

Illustrated Edition — Default, Bankruptcy, Priority, and Real-World Leverage

---

I. Introduction — A UCC Filing Is a Shield, Not a Sword

A UCC-1 does **not** magically enforce itself.
It does **not** seize property automatically.
It does **not** compel repayment by force.

What it *does* is:

✓ Give the secured party **priority rights**
✓ Create enforceable claims **against collateral**
✓ Position the secured party **ahead of others**
✓ Provide legal power in **default and bankruptcy**
✓ Create a pressure tool in **settlement negotiations**
✓ Document ownership interests **in commercial assets**

II. What Happens the Moment a Debtor Defaults

When a debtor fails to perform under the agreement, Article 9 grants the secured party powerful rights:

✓ Right to notify account debtors

✓ Right to collect accounts receivable
✓ Right to repossess certain collateral (if agreed)
✓ Right to render collateral unusable
✓ Right to dispose of collateral commercially
✓ Right to enforce payment
✓ Right to sue for deficiency
✓ Right to block sale or transfer

All of these rights only exist if:

- Attachment occurred
- Perfection is valid
- Priority is intact
- The security agreement supports enforcement

CHAPTER 12

Enforcement Basics & What a UCC Filing REALLY Does in Practice

III. The Security Agreement, Not the UCC-1, Creates Enforcement Power

A UCC-1 **does not** create enforcement rights.

Those rights come from:

1. The **security agreement**
2. Article 9 enforcement provisions

The UCC-1 ONLY:

- Puts the public on notice
- Establishes priority
- Protects against other creditors
- Makes enforcement effective against third parties

Without a security agreement:

❌ No attachment
❌ No enforcement
❌ No repossession
❌ No right to sell collateral

This is why **internal documentation matters.**

"Security Agreement = Power | UCC-1 = Priority"

CHAPTER 12

Enforcement Basics & What a UCC Filing REALLY Does in Practice

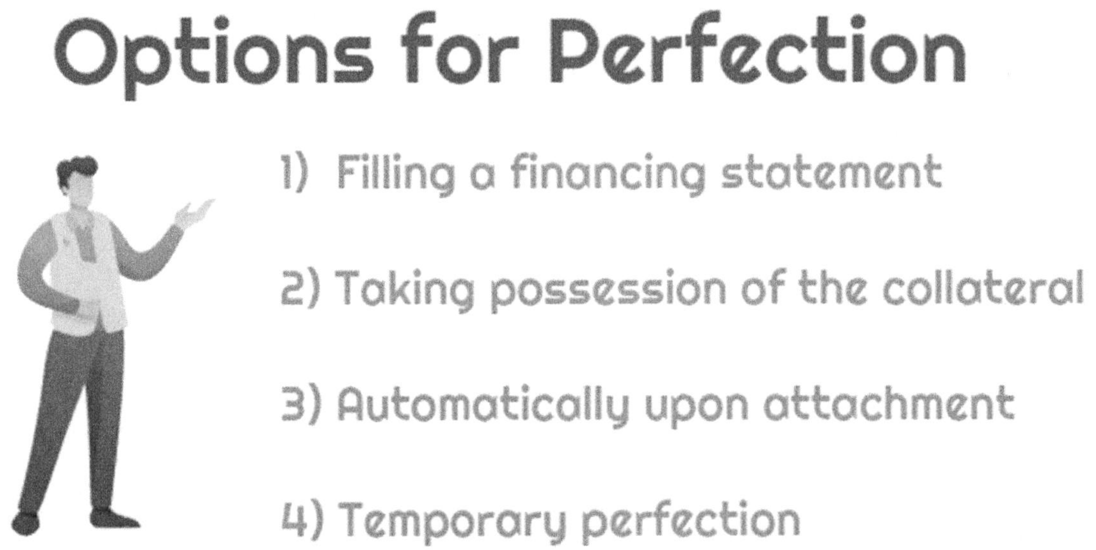

IV. The Enforcement Sequence (The Standard 8-Step Article 9 Process)

Every commercial enforcement follows this order:

1. Default occurs

Debtor fails to perform.

2. Secured Party notifies debtor

Usually required before taking action.

3. Secured Party may notify account debtors

Debtor's customers must pay the secured party directly.

4. Secured Party may repossess collateral

Self-help is allowed *if* peaceful and authorized in agreement.

5. Collateral may be sold or disposed of

Must be "commercially reasonable."

6. Proceeds applied to the debt

Secured party gets paid first.

7. Excess returned to debtor

Required by law.

8. Deficiency may be pursued

CHAPTER 12

Enforcement Basics & What a UCC Filing REALLY Does in Practice

If sale doesn't cover everything.

Below is the visual flow.

V. Enforcement in Bankruptcy — The Power of Priority

Bankruptcy is where UCC filings truly prove their value.

If a debtor files bankruptcy:

✓ A perfected secured party gets paid BEFORE:

- Unsecured creditors
- Contractors
- Employees (in most cases)
- Leaseholders
- Taxing authorities (in many cases)

✓ The secured creditor may even block asset sales

Because their lien must be satisfied first.

Below is the visual.

Image: Bankruptcy Priority Ladder — Where a Perfected Secured Party Stands

CHAPTER 12

Enforcement Basics & What a UCC Filing REALLY Does in Practice

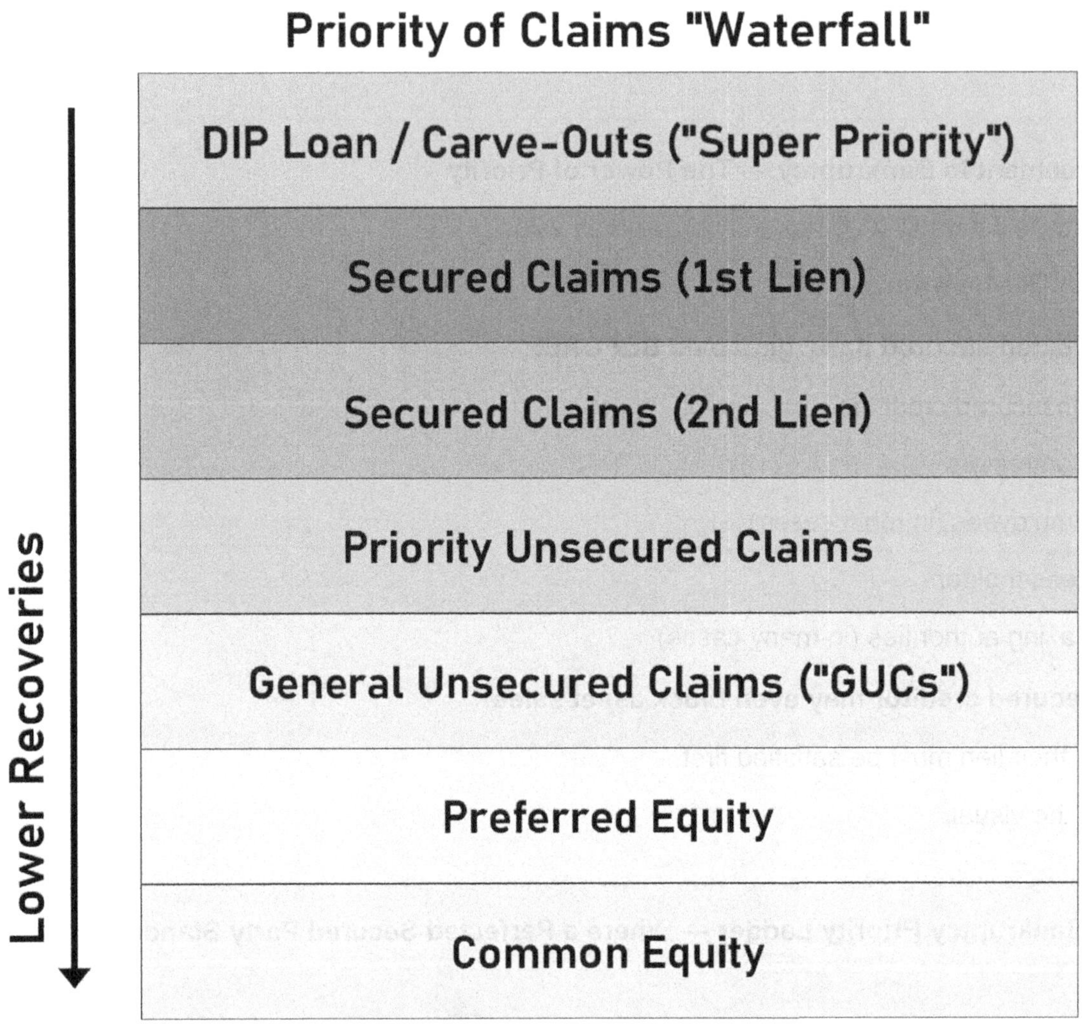

VI. Enforcement Against Competing Creditors (Priority Battles)

When multiple creditors claim the same collateral:

✓ First to file or perfect → WINS

(Unless special rules apply)

This means:

- Even if another creditor has a stronger claim

- Even if the debtor prefers another creditor
- Even if the other creditor lends more money

The one with **earlier perfection** gets paid first.

VII. What Enforcement CANNOT Do

Your guide must maintain legal precision and avoid fringe interpretations.

A UCC filing **cannot**:

❌ Override criminal jurisdiction
❌ Block arrests or detainment
❌ Bind government agencies
❌ Cancel debts unilaterally
❌ Create money
❌ Replace courts
❌ Prevent civil lawsuits
❌ Act as a "super contract"

It ONLY affects:

✓ Collateral
✓ Priority
✓ Commercial rights
✓ Secured creditors
✓ Asset distribution

VIII. Enforcement for Trust-Based Structures (Your Scenario)

Your ecosystem uses:

- **RE 234 270 824 US Holdings** (administrative holding trust)
- **Rodney Cortez Carroll-El Ali Living Trust** (operating trust)
- **Babylon Industries LLC** (commercial entity)

Here's how enforcement plays out:

Scenario:

Babylon Industries LLC defaults on a loan owed to RE 234 270 824 US Holdings.

CHAPTER 12

Enforcement Basics & What a UCC Filing REALLY Does in Practice

Because your filing is:

✓ Perfected
✓ Supported by a security agreement
✓ Demonstrably effective
✓ Properly recorded

The holding trust may enforce by:

✓ Notifying Babylon's customers
✓ Seizing equipment (if agreed)
✓ Collecting accounts receivable
✓ Placing liens on commercial proceeds
✓ Filing a claim in court backed by priority
✓ Blocking transfers of business assets

Below is the visual.

Trust Enforcement Model (Holding Trust → LLC)

CHAPTER 12

Enforcement Basics & What a UCC Filing REALLY Does in Practice

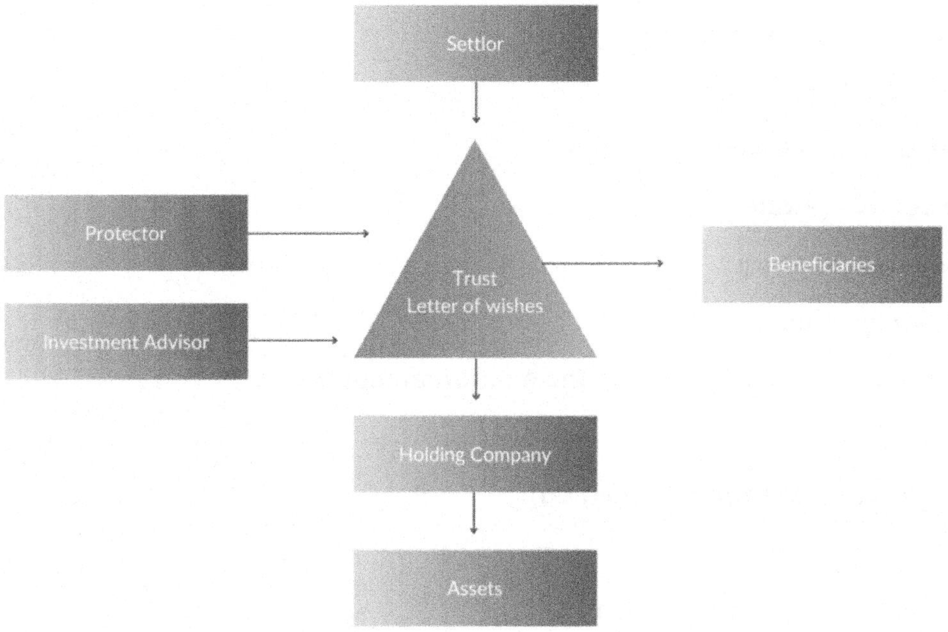

IX. Demonstrating Enforcement Readiness (Your Administrative Power Move)

Courts, creditors, banks, and debtors respect one thing:

Documentation.

To demonstrate you are enforcement-ready:

1. Produce the original UCC-1

Shows priority.

2. Produce all UCC-3s

Shows continuity, assignments, and corrections.

3. Produce the Security Agreement

Shows enforceable rights.

CHAPTER 12

Enforcement Basics & What a UCC Filing REALLY Does in Practice

4. Produce a certified UCC-11

Shows the filing is discoverable.

5. Produce trust resolutions

Shows internal authority to act.

6. Produce administrative notices

Shows the debtor is aware.

7. Produce a ledger entry

Shows value was given.

This creates what courts call a **"prima facie enforcement packet."**

X. Real World Case Example (Simplified)

Scenario

A business defaults on a secured loan.

Outcome

The secured party:

1. Notifies the debtor.
2. Files notice to account debtors.
3. Collects accounts receivable directly.
4. Repossesses certain equipment.
5. Sells collateral commercially.
6. Applies proceeds to the outstanding balance.
7. Pursues deficiency in court.

The court sides entirely with the secured party because:

✓ UCC-1 was perfected
✓ Priority was valid
✓ Collateral was described correctly
✓ Enforcement followed Article 9

CHAPTER 12

Enforcement Basics & What a UCC Filing REALLY Does in Practice

This is how banks and institutions operate daily.

XI. Chapter Summary

Readers now understand:

✓ What enforcement *actually* looks like
✓ How Article 9 protects secured parties
✓ How priority determines who gets paid
✓ How bankruptcy strengthens secured claims
✓ What UCC filings do (and do NOT do)
✓ How to enforce in default
✓ How trusts enforce claims
✓ How to assemble an enforcement packet

This chapter transforms a casual filer into a **professional secured creditor**.

CHAPTER 13

Advanced Filing Structures: Multi-Debtor, Multi-Secured Party & Cross-Collateralization Models

Illustrated Edition — High-Level Structuring for Trusts, Corporations, and Complex Estates

---

I. Introduction — Why Advanced Structures Matter

Real-world secured transactions are rarely simple.

Sophisticated entities use:

- **Multiple debtors**
- **Multiple secured parties**
- **Stacked collateral layers**
- **Holding-trust structures**
- **Cross-collateral guarantees**
- **Multi-entity financing webs**

These structures increase:

✓ Asset protection
✓ Administrative control
✓ Estate-level leverage
✓ Commercial flexibility
✓ Enforcement options
✓ Negotiation strength

CHAPTER 13

Advanced Filing Structures: Multi-Debtor, Multi-Secured Party & Cross-Collateralization Models

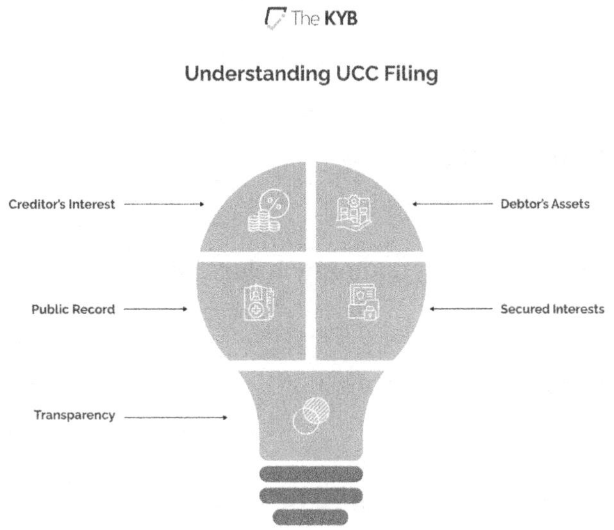

II. Multi-Debtor Structures — When More Than One Party Owes the Obligation

A multi-debtor filing arises when:

- Two businesses jointly borrow
- A trust guarantees an LLC
- A parent company and subsidiary co-sign
- Two individuals co-own collateral
- A trust and beneficiary share obligations

Each debtor must be listed **exactly**.

✓ Each debtor's assets become subject to the lien

✓ Each debtor is searchable in the database

✓ Each debtor can be enforced separately

Example:
Babylon Industries LLC and a new subsidiary, Babylon Freight LLC, jointly borrow from RE 234 270 824 US Holdings.

A. Types of Multi-Debtor Arrangements

CHAPTER 13

Advanced Filing Structures: Multi-Debtor, Multi-Secured Party & Cross-Collateralization Models

1. Joint Debtors

Both are equally responsible.

2. Debtor + Guarantor

One is primary debtor; one guarantees.

3. Parent–Subsidiary Structure

Holding company guarantees operating company collateral.

4. Trust–LLC Hybrid

Trust owns collateral; LLC controls operations.

III. Multi-Secured Party Structures — Shared or Tiered Claims

Sometimes more than one secured party files **the same financing statement**.

This occurs in:

- Syndicated loans
- Trust co-administration
- Multi-trust ownership
- Commercial partnerships
- Layered estate protection

✓ All secured parties must be listed

✓ They share or divide enforcement rights

✓ Their internal agreement governs priority between them

A. Forms of Multi-Secured Party Structures

1. Equal Shared Priority (Syndication)

Each secured party has equal standing.

2. Senior–Junior Priority (Private Agreement)

Private contract controls priority between secured parties.

CHAPTER 13

Advanced Filing Structures: Multi-Debtor, Multi-Secured Party & Cross-Collateralization Models

3. Distributed Collateral Rights

Trust A: Accounts
Trust B: Equipment
Trust C: IP

4. Multi-Trust Administrative Web

Used for estate systems like yours.

IV. Cross-Collateralization — One Collateral Pool Secures Multiple Obligations

This is one of the most powerful advanced tools.

Cross-collateralization means:

✓ One asset can secure multiple loans

✓ Multiple assets can secure one loan
✓ A trust estate can secure multiple obligations
✓ A single filing can support layered agreements

For example:

- Babylon Industries LLC pledges equipment as collateral
- That same collateral supports **two** financing arrangements:
    - One with RE 234 270 824 US Holdings
    - One internally with the Rodney Cortez Carroll-El Ali Living Trust

---

V. Multi-Layer Trust Structures (Modeled on YOUR System)

Holding Trust → Operating Trust → LLC

Your structure is an ideal teaching model:

Secured Party #1:

RE 234 270 824 US Holdings (Holding Trust)

Secured Party #2:

Rodney Cortez Carroll-El Ali Living Trust (Operating Trust)

Debtor:

CHAPTER 13

Advanced Filing Structures: Multi-Debtor, Multi-Secured Party & Cross-Collateralization Models

Babylon Industries LLC

This allows:

✓ Administrative control
✓ Estate integrity
✓ Revenue and equipment separation
✓ Multi-layer enforcement
✓ Superior protection against outside creditors

Below is your custom visual.

Three-Tier Trust Collateral System

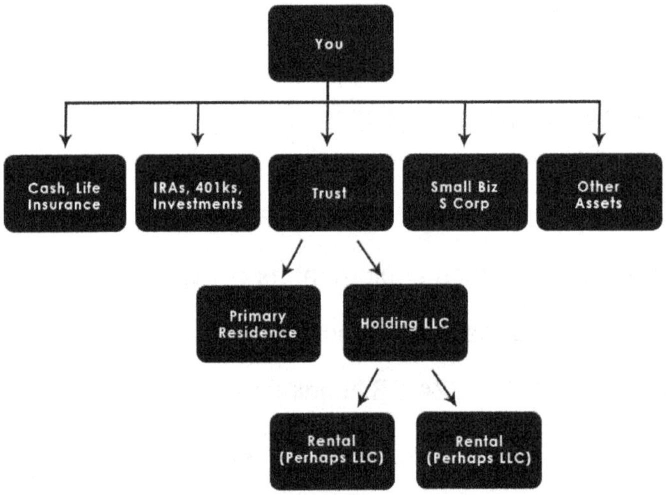

VI. Cross-Default Clauses — Linking Multiple Agreements

A cross-default clause means:

Default in one agreement = default in ALL linked agreements.

This gives the secured party or trust system:

✓ Maximum leverage
✓ Faster enforcement
✓ Greater protection
✓ A unified administrative framework

Example:

CHAPTER 13

Advanced Filing Structures: Multi-Debtor, Multi-Secured Party & Cross-Collateralization Models

If Babylon Industries LLC defaults on a loan from the Holding Trust, it may automatically default on a separate financing arrangement with the Living Trust.

VII. Cross-Collateral vs. Cross-Default — They Are NOT the Same

Cross-Collateral

Several obligations share the same collateral.

Cross-Default

Default on one triggers default on the others.

Using them together creates:

Maximum estate leverage + maximum creditor control.

VIII. Interlocking Filings — Multiple UCC Filings Supporting One Structure

Advanced estate or business structures often use:

- Several UCC-1 filings
- Assigned interests
- Overlapping collateral categories
- Multi-party loan documents
- Tiered entity control

For example:

UCC-1 #1:
Living Trust → LLC (equipment, inventory)

UCC-1 #2:
Holding Trust → LLC (accounts, general intangibles)

UCC-1 #3:
Holding Trust → Living Trust (beneficial interests, proceeds)

This creates a **web of administrative control**.

Interlocking UCC Filings Web

CHAPTER 13

Advanced Filing Structures: Multi-Debtor, Multi-Secured Party & Cross-Collateralization Models

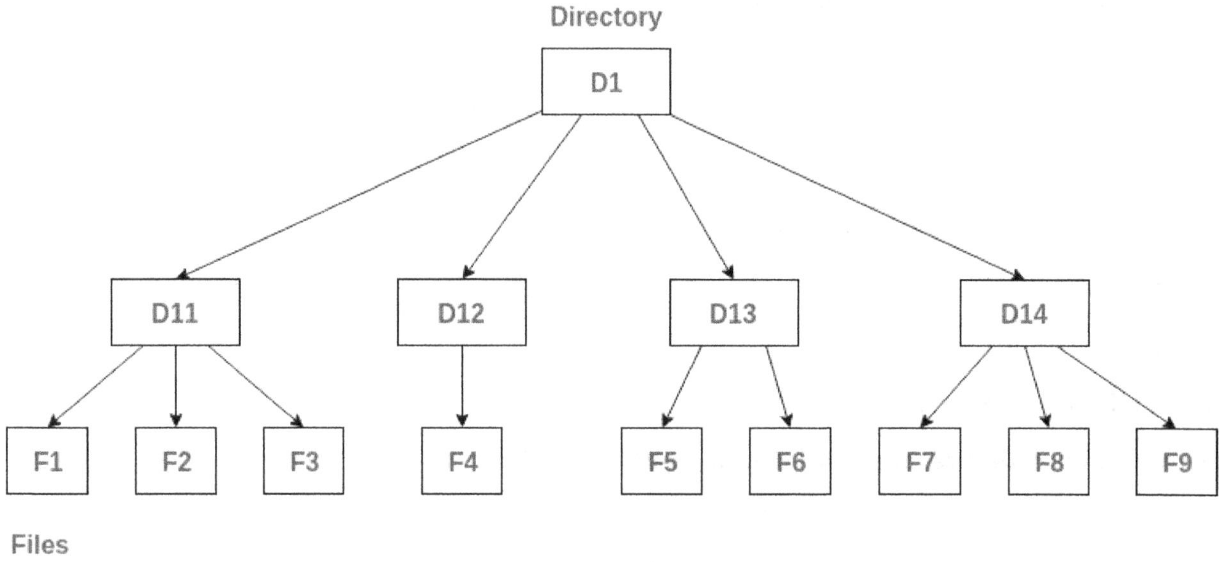

IX. Multi-Party Enforcement Rights — How Defaults Are Managed

With multiple secured parties:

- Each party may enforce independently
- Or one party (administrative trust) controls enforcement
- Parties may enforce sequentially or collectively
- Priority rules remain intact

Your structure example:

If Babylon Industries LLC defaults:

- RE 234 270 824 US Holdings (Holding Trust) enforces primary rights
- Rodney Cortez Carroll-El Ali Living Trust enforces secondary internal rights

X. Demonstrating Effectiveness of Complex Structures

The more complex the filing, the more critical it is to **prove** legal effectiveness.

Your demonstration packet should include:

1. All UCC-1 filings

CHAPTER 13

Advanced Filing Structures: Multi-Debtor, Multi-Secured Party & Cross-Collateralization Models

2. All UCC-3 amendments
3. Assignments transferring interests
4. Trust resolutions authorizing filings
5. Security agreements for each loan
6. Cross-default agreements
7. Cross-collateral schedules
8. Certified UCC-11 searches showing all filings
9. Administrative binders documenting value given

XI. Chapter Summary

Readers now understand:

✓ Multi-debtor structures
✓ Multi-secured-party structures
✓ Cross-collateralization strategies
✓ Cross-default clauses
✓ Interlocking UCC filings
✓ Multi-trust and LLC arrangements
✓ How to preserve priority in complex setups
✓ How to enforce across multiple entities
✓ How to demonstrate effectiveness of advanced structures

This chapter transforms the guidebook from *standard* to **professional-level**, suitable for real enterprise and trust administrators.

CHAPTER 14

Trust-Based UCC Strategies & Administrative Integration

Illustrated Edition — How Trusts Use Article 9 to Secure, Control, and Manage Assets

---

I. Introduction — Why Trusts Are Exceptional Secured Parties

Trusts are **not corporations**, **not individuals**, and **not government entities**.

They are **private legal arrangements** that:

✓ Own property
✓ Issue authority through trustees
✓ Hold equitable and legal interests
✓ Maintain internal minutes & resolutions
✓ Operate outside typical commercial frameworks

Trusts use UCC filings to:

- Document ownership of collateral
- Secure beneficial interests
- Control assets across LLCs & subsidiaries
- Establish administrative priority
- Create enforceable internal and external claims
- Build layered estate structures

CHAPTER 14

Trust-Based UCC Strategies & Administrative Integration

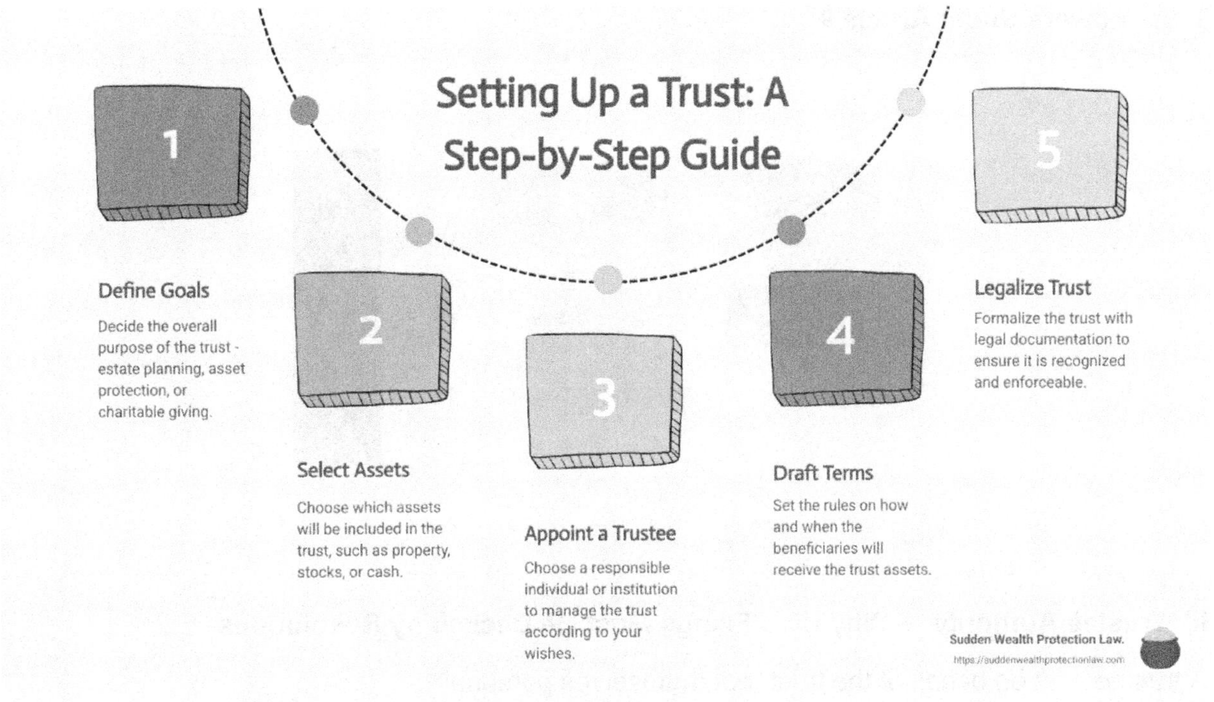

II. The Trust as Secured Party — Legal Definition and Powers

A trust may act as a secured party when:

1. A trustee signs a **security agreement**
2. The trust is properly named as secured party
3. The trust holds a lawful claim or beneficial interest
4. The trustee issues an administrative resolution authorizing action

Trust Powers Under Article 9:

✓ Perfect security interests
✓ Enforce secured claims
✓ Assign security interests
✓ Maintain priority over decades
✓ Use trust assets to support obligations
✓ Receive collateral or proceeds

Below is the visual.

CHAPTER 14

Trust-Based UCC Strategies & Administrative Integration

Trust Powers Under Article 9

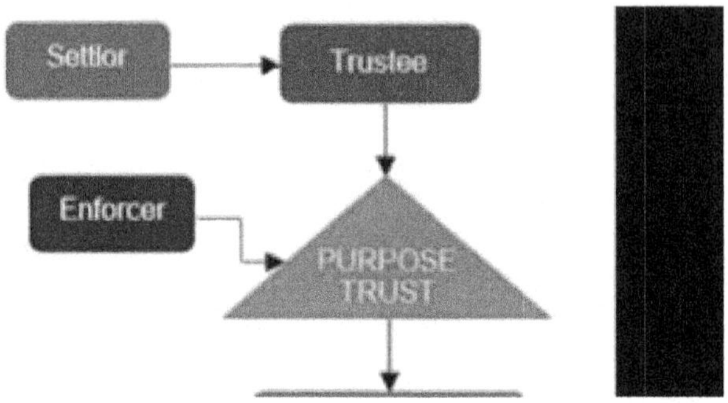

III. Trustee Authority — Why UCC Filings Must Be Backed by Resolutions

A trustee acts on behalf of the trust, not themselves personally.

Every UCC filing should be supported by:

1. **Minutes** — documenting the meeting or decision
2. **Resolution** — formally authorizing the filing
3. **Schedule A/B/C** — detailing the collateral involved
4. **Administrative ledger** — showing value given

These documents build a **legal chain of authority** that courts respect.

Below is the visual.

"Chain of Authority" — Trustee → Trust → Filing

CHAPTER 14

Trust-Based UCC Strategies & Administrative Integration

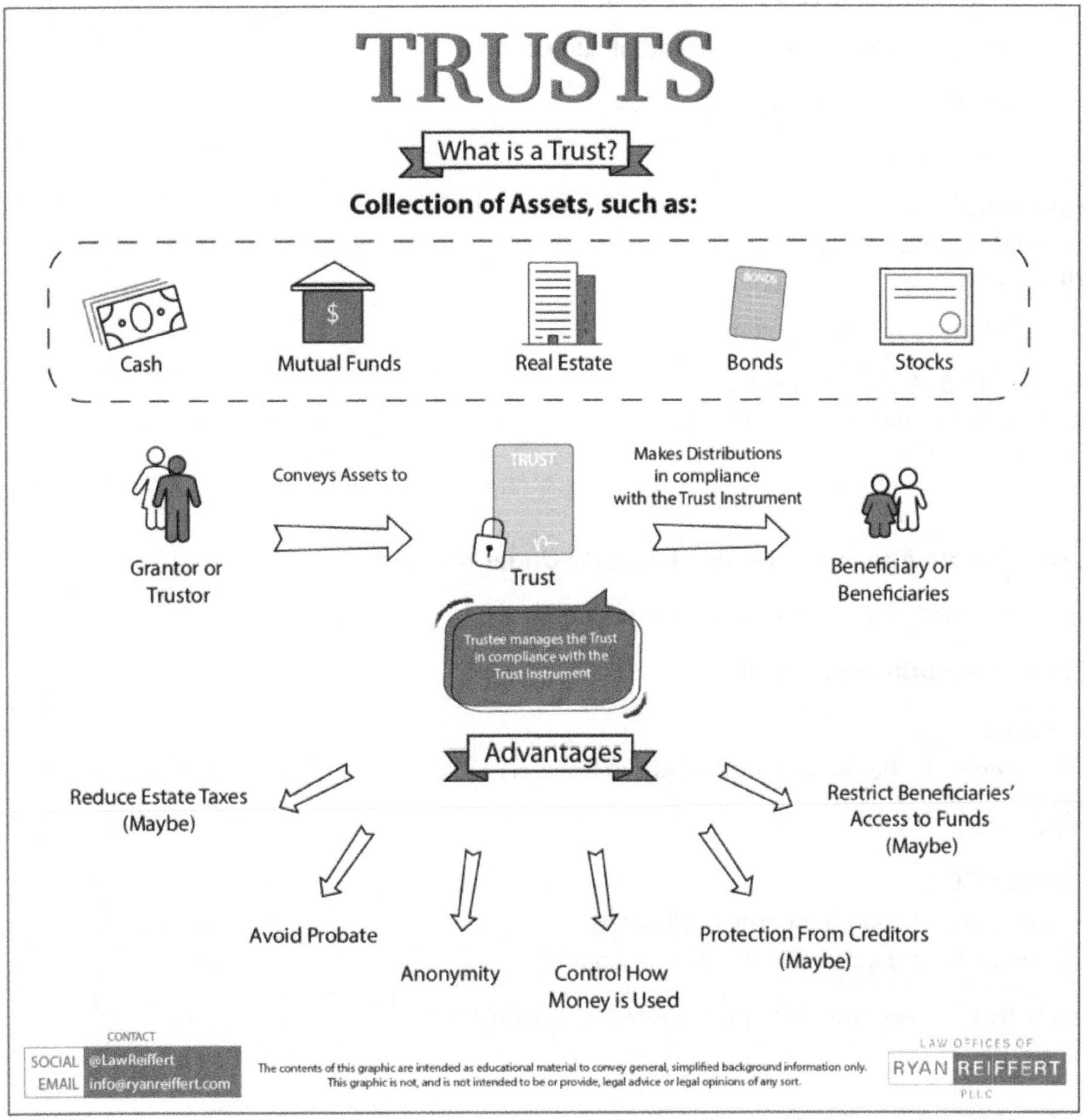

IV. Naming the Trust Correctly (Critical for Acceptance & Searchability)

Most UCC rejections involving trusts occur because:

- The trust's legal name was incorrect

CHAPTER 14

Trust-Based UCC Strategies & Administrative Integration

- The trustee was listed instead of the trust
- The trust was described instead of named
- Improper abbreviations were used

The correct format is:

Trust Name
c/o **Trustee Name**, Trustee
Trust Address

Example (based on your system):

RE 234 270 824 US Holdings
c/o Rodney Cortez Carroll™, Trustee
(Trust Address)

V. How Trusts Attach and Perfect Interests Under Article 9

To legally attach a security interest, the trust must:

✓ **Have a security agreement**

✓ Provide value
✓ Have rights in the collateral (or power to transfer)

To perfect:

✓ File a UCC-1
✓ Or take possession (for certain collateral)
✓ Or control (for deposit & investment accounts)

This is **trust-based attachment**, not individual attachment.

VI. Trust Minutes & Resolutions — Required Internal Documentation

Every trust UCC filing should include a private administrative record:

Required Components:

- Trustee oath or acceptance
- Trust minutes documenting the decision
- Resolution authorizing the filing

CHAPTER 14

Trust-Based UCC Strategies & Administrative Integration

- Schedule A (collateral list)
- Ledger entry showing consideration
- Administrative certificate of authority

This internal documentation:

✓ Demonstrates lawful basis
✓ Establishes attachment
✓ Reduces disputes
✓ Strengthens enforcement
✓ Protects trustees legally

VII. Multi-Trust Administrative Ecosystems (Your System Modeled)

Your structure is an ideal high-level teaching example:

Tier 1 — Administrative Holding Trust:

RE 234 270 824 US Holdings
(Controls secured interests)

Tier 2 — Living/Operating Trust:

Rodney Cortez Carroll-El Ali Living Trust
(Holds beneficial and operational interests)

Tier 3 — LLC Layer:

Babylon Industries LLC
(Commercial operations)

This creates:

✓ Asset separation
✓ Liability insulation
✓ Interlocking secured rights
✓ Administrative continuity

CHAPTER 14

Trust-Based UCC Strategies & Administrative Integration

Hierarchy of Trust

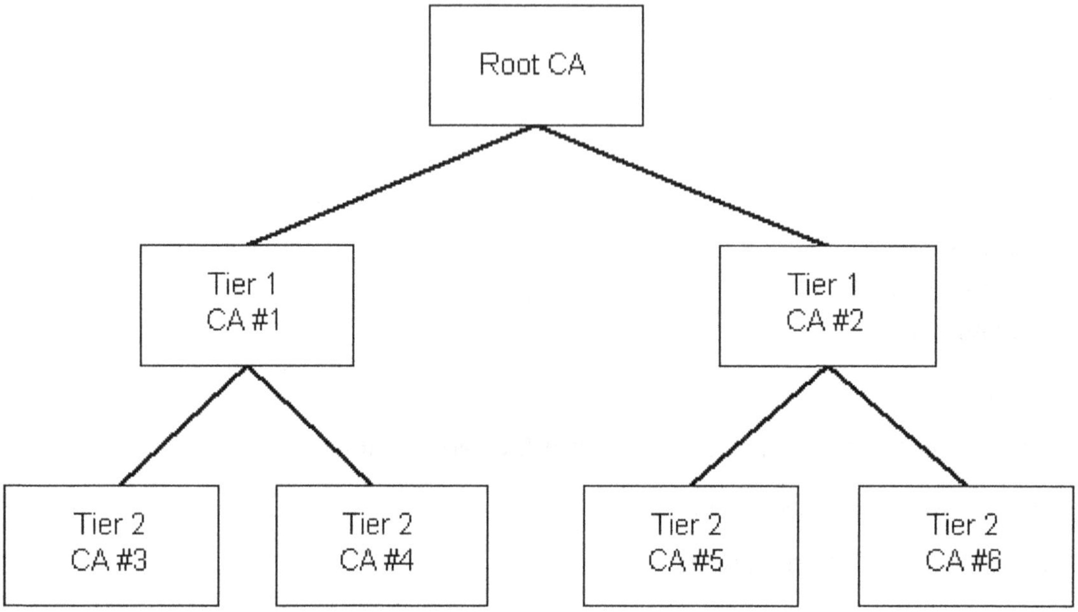

VIII. Cross-Collateralization Inside Trust Systems

Trusts can:

✓ Secure LLC assets
✓ Secure beneficiary obligations
✓ Secure internal loans
✓ Secure external debt
✓ Use one filing to support multiple agreements
✓ Use multiple filings to support one agreement

This creates a **web of administrative control** for estate management.

IX. Using Assignments to Move Secured Rights Between Trusts

Assignments allow trusts to:

- Consolidate control
- Transfer secured rights during leadership changes

CHAPTER 14

Trust-Based UCC Strategies & Administrative Integration

- Move collateral between trusts
- Support estate restructuring
- Maintain continuity across generations

Your example:

Living Trust → Holding Trust
(via UCC-3 Assignment)

This is standard in professional trust administration.

Below is the visual.

X. Demonstrating Trust Filing Effectiveness (Court & Agency Ready)

To prove a trust UCC filing is valid:

Produce the following:

1. The original UCC-1
2. All UCC-3 amendments
3. Trust minutes authorizing the filing
4. A certified UCC-11 search
5. A valid security agreement
6. Schedule A listing collateral
7. Ledger entry proving consideration
8. Trustee certificate of authority

Courts LOVE:

- A clean chain of authority
- A clean chain of documentation
- A clean chain of filings

Below is the visual.

CHAPTER 14

Trust-Based UCC Strategies & Administrative Integration

SECURED PARTY PACKAGE OUTLINE

FAST TRACK

What is a Secured Party Creditor?

Secured Party Creditor ("SPC") – someone who was a Corporate Citizen and has a birth certificate or Certificate of Citizenship (if born abroad), or permanent resident who has a green card and social security number; who has voided and canceled the contracts creating the U.S. Citizen/Resident, and replaced them with a Private Citizen status who also has taken control of their LEGAL NAME trust, and can operate freely to discharge debts or court actions at will.

The Process of Becoming One: "Taking Back Your Rights"

1. **Authenticate The Birth Certificate: "Should we or Should We not?" YOU Decide By reading the Extensive Break down in the Link Below** *https://www.scribd.com/doc/251392513/Authenticating-the-Birth-Certificate*
2. **Copywrite/Trademark your Name By filing it with the "Real Properties" division in your local County Clerks office. (Template:** https://drive.google.com/file/d/0B0tJIYKPFQ-8ZDJVdHlfWVZmU28/view?usp=sharing)

3. **Record a Document of Title: File *Affidavit of Beneficial Ownership* (Document) with Local Count Clerk "Real Properties" Division.** (https://drive.google.com/file/d/0B0tJIYKPFQ-8dkZtZEV0Vk9zdzg/view?usp=sharing)

4. **Record the Name & *Title of Memorandum* for your Foreign Situs Trust (John Alex Doe El Trust Under Declaration of Trust X-XX-XXXX)** (https://drive.google.com/file/d/0B0tJIYKPFQ-8TnM3dHZ4VEhlMm8/view?usp=sharing)

5. **Moors Record *Judicial Name and Proclamation Notice* on Public Record**
   (https://drive.google.com/file/d/0B0tJIYKPFQ-8UkQ2QzAwa0dkakE/view?usp=sharing)
   (https://drive.google.com/file/d/0B0tJIYKPFQ-8X0xScjRqSGJsd3M/view?usp=sharing)
   G
6. **Apply for Foreign Identification Numbers EIN #s: The Purpose of This form is to establish a foreign trust that is tax-exempt and is foreign to U.S. jurisdiction.**
   Instructions:
   - **Fill out the form with your personal information following the example BELOW.**
   - **Call IRS at 1-267-941-1000 or 1-267-941-1099.**
   - **They may require you to fax over SS-4 form, be prepared.**
   - **You are the trustee.**
   - **IRS will try to add the word TRUST after your name. This is not acceptable you must have the 98-Series trust needs to be just your name. Tell the IRS agent the TRUST has already been created, it is about to receive income. If the IRS can not provide an EIN # for your name as the trust, than request a letter from them that this entity is tax exempt and not required to file taxes.**

- **Erect a Foreign "82-Estate Number" (Explanation In Video at 4:00 Minute mark – (https://www.youtube.com/watch?v=jgA2ISsJ3gI&feature=youtu.be)**
- **Complete a SS4 Document to Establish a "98-Foreign Corporate Number". This Trust number will be used to "Do Business" and open bank accounts under your Foreign Identity. (SS4 Corporate Example -** https://drive.google.com/file/d/0B0tJIYKPFQ-8VTRUYlhiZzhza2s/view?usp=sharing)
- **Complete another SS4 Document Establishing your main "98 Foreign Situs TRUST" Identity, titled "John Alex Doe El Trust". This Foreign Situs Trust will embody All of your "Personal" affairs (Strawman Files, 82 Estate, Corporate Estate). Meaning all of your Personal Property is now "Held in a Trust" privately under the foreign control of your situs trust. (SS4 Example -** https://drive.google.com/file/d/0B0tJIYKPFQ-8UFVad3hlQ0NSSGc/view?

XI. Why Trust-Based UCC Strategies Are Superior to Personal Filings

CHAPTER 14

Trust-Based UCC Strategies & Administrative Integration

✓ They survive death

✓ They survive bankruptcy (most structures)

✓ They maintain administrative continuity

✓ They reduce personal liability

✓ They support generational estate planning

✓ They allow tiered secured interests

✓ They protect operating businesses

✓ They integrate perfectly with UCC systems

Trusts allow a person to operate like a:

- Private lender
- Estate administrator
- Commercial creditor
- Asset protector
- Secured party with multi-generational reach

XII. Chapter Summary

Readers now understand:

✓ How trusts act as secured parties
✓ How trustees authorize UCC filings
✓ How to maintain a trust administrative record
✓ How to attach and perfect interests correctly
✓ How multi-trust ecosystems interact
✓ How to structure trust–LLC collateral webs
✓ How to demonstrate trust filing effectiveness
✓ How trust filings support generational estate planning

This chapter makes the entire UCC system *practical* for estate-level strategies.

CHAPTER 15

Real Property Interfaces: What UCC Filings Can and Cannot Do With Land, Homes & Title Instruments

Illustrated Edition — UCC Article 9 vs. Real Estate Law (Fixtures, Land, Leaseholds & Trust Integration)

I. Introduction — The Border Between "Personal Property" and "Real Property"

The UCC governs **personal property**, not **real estate**.

But certain assets connected to real estate — like **fixtures** — fall under Article 9.
This creates a hybrid zone where Article 9 *interacts* with real property law.

Your readers must understand:

✓ What CAN be secured in a UCC filing
✓ What CANNOT be secured
✓ Which filings must go to the **county recorder**
✓ Which filings stay in the **Secretary of State**
✓ How land-related interests can be perfected

CHAPTER 15

Real Property Interfaces: What UCC Filings Can and Cannot Do With Land, Homes & Title Instruments

"UCC vs Real Property" — Side-by-Side Jurisdiction Breakdown

CHAPTER 15

Real Property Interfaces: What UCC Filings Can and Cannot Do With Land, Homes & Title Instruments

PERSONAL PROPERTY

Everything that is not real estate is considered PERSONAL PROPERTY.

PERSONAL PROPERTY is also known as CHATTEL

As a general rule of thumb, that which is MOVABLE is considered personal property.

FURNITURE APPLIANCES MOVABLE SHELVES TELEVISION DRESSER

TRADE FIXTURE

Items that are installed by a business or commercial tenant and are removable upon termination of the tenancy.

Trade fixtures are considered PERSONAL PROPERTY of the tenant.

BUSINESS SIGNAGE DISPLAY COUNTERS CUSTOM EQUIPMENT STORE SHELVES

EMBLEMENTS

The crops and other annual plantings grown on a property (farm) are considered to be personal property of the cultivator.

CORN APPLES POTATOES STRAWBERRIES

RealEstateU®

CHAPTER 15

Real Property Interfaces: What UCC Filings Can and Cannot Do With Land, Homes & Title Instruments

II. What UCC Filings *CANNOT* Cover

Your guide must be crystal-clear.

A UCC-1 cannot:

✕ Secure ownership of land
✕ Replace a deed or title
✕ Encumber real estate directly
✕ Override county-level recording laws
✕ Change zoning or county records
✕ Act as a mortgage or deed of trust
✕ Remove property from taxation
✕ Convey real property rights

Real estate rights are governed by:

- State property statutes
- County title systems
- Deeds
- Mortgages
- Land records

Article 9 does NOT touch these.

III. What UCC Filings *CAN* Secure Related to Real Property

Although UCC filings cannot secure land, they *can* secure interests tied to land, such as:

✓ Fixtures

Items attached to real property.

✓ Growing crops

Treated as goods under the UCC.

✓ Manufactured homes (when classified as personal property)

Before they are legally converted to real estate.

CHAPTER 15

Real Property Interfaces: What UCC Filings Can and Cannot Do With Land, Homes & Title Instruments

✓ **Extraction rights (oil, gas, minerals)**

When treated as personal property pre-extraction.

✓ **Leasehold interests (depending on jurisdiction)**

Especially equipment or improvements made by the tenant.

✓ **Payment streams related to real estate**

Such as rents, receivables, and security deposits.

IV. What Is a "Fixture" Under Article 9?

Fixtures are personal property that become part of real property due to:

- Attachment
- Adaptation
- Intent to permanently affix

Examples:

✓ Central HVAC systems
✓ Built-in shelving
✓ Industrial machinery bolted to floors
✓ Solar panel installations
✓ Commercial refrigeration systems

Fixtures are secured through a **Fixture Filing**, not a standard UCC-1.

V. Fixture Filings — How They Work

A **Fixture Filing** is a UCC filing made in the **county land records**, NOT at the Secretary of State.

A proper fixture filing must include:

1. **UCC-1 formatted as a Fixture Filing**
2. **Debtor name**
3. **Secured party name**

CHAPTER 15

Real Property Interfaces: What UCC Filings Can and Cannot Do With Land, Homes & Title Instruments

4. **Description of real property**
5. **Record owner if different from debtor**
6. **Collateral description identifying fixtures**

Location:
County Recorder or Land Records Office where the property is located.

VI. Real Property Description Requirements

Unlike standard UCC filings, fixture filings must identify the real property.

Examples include:

- Lot and block numbers
- Legal description
- Township/range/section
- Parcel number

The legal description must match **county title records**.

VII. UCC Filings and Manufactured Housing (Important)

Manufactured homes live in a legal gray zone.

They are:

- Personal property BEFORE conversion
- Real property AFTER being permanently affixed + recorded as real estate

UCC Filing Allowed When:

✓ The manufactured home is still titled
✓ Not yet converted to real property
✓ Not yet recorded on the land deed

UCC Filing NOT Allowed When:

CHAPTER 15

Real Property Interfaces: What UCC Filings Can and Cannot Do With Land, Homes & Title Instruments

✗ The home has been legally converted to real estate
✗ The title has been surrendered
✗ County has recorded it as part of land

VIII. Trust Integration — Holding Real Property & UCC Interests

Trusts can hold:

✓ Land
✓ Buildings
✓ Fixtures
✓ LLC membership interests in property companies

Trusts can also:

✓ File fixture filings
✓ Claim security interests in fixtures
✓ Secure equipment located on land
✓ Secure rent streams
✓ Secure tenant improvements

Example Using Your Structure:

RE 234 270 824 US Holdings
→ Holds title to a property

Rodney Cortez Carroll-El Ali Living Trust
→ Holds a UCC interest in tenant improvements, machinery, or rental proceeds

Babylon Industries LLC
→ Operates the commercial activity on the land

This creates:

✓ Multiple layers of protection
✓ Administrative control
✓ Trust-centered asset architecture

CHAPTER 15

Real Property Interfaces: What UCC Filings Can and Cannot Do With Land, Homes & Title Instruments

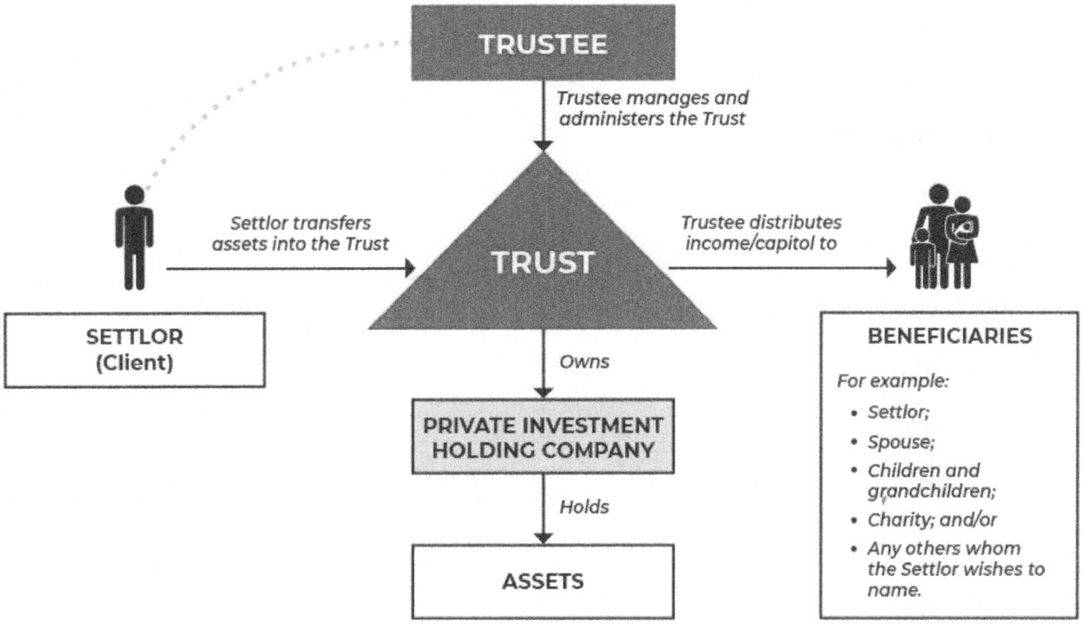

IX. Securing Rents, Leases & Income Streams

Even though you cannot secure **real property**, you can secure:

✓ Rent payments
✓ Lease income
✓ Tenant payments
✓ Royalty streams
✓ Proceeds from land-based operations

These are **personal property rights**, not real estate.

X. Using UCC Filings in Real Estate Business Structures

Real estate investors often use UCC filings to secure:

- Property management receivables

CHAPTER 15

Real Property Interfaces: What UCC Filings Can and Cannot Do With Land, Homes & Title Instruments

- Construction equipment
- Contractor agreements
- Leasehold improvements
- Solar installations
- Airbnb furnishings
- Short-term rental equipment
- Water rights (pre-extraction)
- Timber rights

Trusts use Article 9 to separate:

- Ownership
- Control
- Collateralization
- Income streams

CHAPTER 15

Real Property Interfaces: What UCC Filings Can and Cannot Do With Land, Homes & Title Instruments

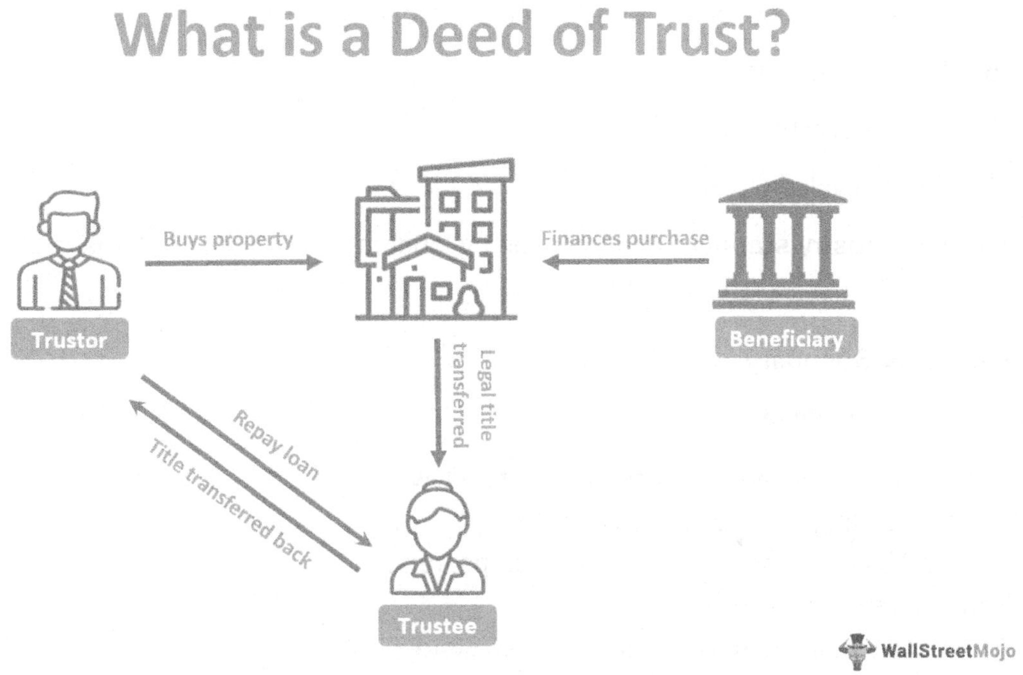

XI. Common Mistakes to Avoid in Real Property UCC Filings

❌ Filing a standard UCC-1 against land
❌ Attempting to "UCC lien a house"
❌ Filing at the wrong location (SOS vs. county)
❌ Failing to include the real property description
❌ Failing to identify the record owner
❌ Using UCC filings for deeds, titles, or land patents
❌ Attempting to bypass real estate law with UCC instruments

XII. Demonstrating Effectiveness of Real Property-Related UCC Filings

To show that a fixture filing or related UCC filing is valid:

Produce:

1. The UCC fixture filing with recording stamp
2. The underlying security agreement
3. A certified UCC search

4. The deed or county record (proof of real property identity)
5. Trust resolutions
6. Collateral schedule
7. Proof of value given

This is the **industry standard** method used by lenders, developers, and trust administrators.

XIII. Chapter Summary

Readers now understand:

✓ The boundary between UCC and real estate law
✓ What UCC filings cannot secure (land)
✓ What UCC filings can secure (fixtures, crops, rent, etc.)
✓ How fixture filings work
✓ When to file at the county vs. Secretary of State
✓ How manufactured housing interacts with UCC law
✓ How trusts integrate land holdings and UCC collateral
✓ How to avoid improper filings
✓ How to demonstrate effectiveness

This chapter protects your readers from the most common UCC misunderstanding in America.

CHAPTER 16

UCC Filing Audits, Maintenance & Long-Term Administrative Strategy

I. Introduction — UCC Filings Are Not "Set and Forget"

A UCC filing system must be **maintained**, just like:

- Accounting records
- Real estate holdings
- Corporate books
- Trust minutes
- State registrations

Without maintenance, filings:

❌ Lapse
❌ Lose priority
❌ Become unsearchable
❌ Conflict with updated names
❌ Overlap improperly with other filings

This chapter teaches **how to prevent failure** and **maintain perfection** for decades.

II. The 3-Pillar System of UCC Maintenance

A long-term secured-creditor system requires:

✔ Pillar 1 — Annual Administrative Audit

Review all filings, agreements, and administrative records.

✔ Pillar 2 — Calendarized Continuation Schedule

Track all 5-year expiration windows.

✔ Pillar 3 — Debtor Search Monitoring

Run periodic searches to detect unauthorized filings or changes.

III. Annual UCC Administrative Audit (Professional Standard)

Every year, trust administrators and corporate finance departments do a **UCC Annual Audit** consisting of:

1. Verify Debtor Name Accuracy

CHAPTER 16

UCC Filing Audits, Maintenance & Long-Term Administrative Strategy

Has the debtor:

- Changed legal name?
- Converted entities?
- Merged or dissolved?
- Changed addresses?

If yes → **Amend UCC-1**.

2. Verify Secured Party Information

Has the secured party:

- Assigned rights?
- Changed name?
- Moved jurisdiction?

If yes → update filings and trust records.

3. Verify Collateral Schedules

Confirm:

- Collateral still exists
- Collateral has not been sold
- Collateral descriptions remain accurate

4. Verify Underlying Agreements

Ensure:

- Contracts support the filings
- Trust resolutions are in order
- Ledgers reflect consideration

5. Verify Filing Status

Ensure no:

- Unauthorized amendments
- Fraudulent terminations
- Duplicate filings

CHAPTER 16

UCC Filing Audits, Maintenance & Long-Term Administrative Strategy

IV. Continuation Calendar System (5-Year Rule Management)

Every UCC-1 expires after **5 years** unless continued within the **6-month window**.

Build a system that tracks:

✓ Filing date
✓ Expiration date
✓ Continuation window
✓ Assignments or amendments
✓ Responsible trustee or officer

Industry Standard:
Track continuation deadlines **36 months, 48 months, and 54 months** after filing.

This gives:

- Plenty of lead time
- Backup time
- Administrative redundancy

V. Debtor Search Monitoring (Fraud Detection & Compliance)

Every 6–12 months, you must:

✓ Run a UCC-11 Search on the Debtor

This detects:

- New creditor claims
- Fraudulent terminations
- Overlapping collateral claims
- Debtor reorganizations
- Undisclosed secured parties

✓ Run a UCC Search on the Secured Party

This detects:

- Conflicts with your name

- Fraudulently assigned interests
- Unwanted cross-filings

VI. Filing Synchronization Across Entities (Trust & LLC Alignment)

In multi-entity systems like yours, filings must be synchronized across:

- Holding trusts
- Operating trusts
- LLCs
- Subsidiaries
- DBAs
- Affiliates

Why synchronization matters:

✓ Prevents cross-collateral conflicts
✓ Ensures correct priority order
✓ Maintains administrative clarity
✓ Avoids inconsistent debtor names
✓ Ensures collateral is accurately assigned

VII. Internal Trust Administrative Cycle (Your System Model)

Your trust ecosystem involves:

Tier 1 — RE 234 270 824 US Holdings (NGO Holding Trust)

✓ Oversees secured interests
✓ Files UCC-1s
✓ Manages assignments
✓ Maintains administrative ledger

Tier 2 — Rodney Cortez Carroll-El Ali Living Trust

CHAPTER 16

UCC Filing Audits, Maintenance & Long-Term Administrative Strategy

✓ Holds operational beneficial interests
✓ Secures internal obligations
✓ Issues trustee resolutions

Tier 3 — Babylon Industries LLC

✓ Acts as commercial debtor
✓ Generates accounts, receivables, equipment

A long-term administrative cycle should include:

1. Quarterly review of internal ledgers
2. Annual trust resolution updates
3. Annual UCC filing audit
4. 5-year continuation scheduling
5. Cross-checking collateral schedules
6. Updating trust certificates of authority

VIII. The "Master Filing Log" — The Core of Long-Term Administration

A Master Filing Log contains:

- Filing number
- Filing date
- Expiration date
- Collateral categories
- Debtor entity
- Secured party entity
- Link to underlying agreement
- Continuation window dates
- Notes on assignments or amendments

Maintained digitally and on paper, this becomes your **administrative Bible**.

CHAPTER 16

UCC Filing Audits, Maintenance & Long-Term Administrative Strategy

IX. Multi-Entity Continuity Planning (Avoiding Administrative Collapse)

What happens if:

- The trustee becomes incapacitated?
- An LLC dissolves?
- A trust transitions to successor trustees?
- A business restructures?
- A filing is overlooked?

A continuity plan must include:

✓ Automatic successor trustee authority
✓ Perpetual administrative resolutions
✓ Documented assignment procedures
✓ Emergency filing instructions
✓ A successor administrative binder
✓ Duplicate filing logs stored externally

X. Detecting and Responding to Administrative Threats

Administrative threats include:

- Fraudulent terminations
- Unauthorized amendments
- Debtor name changes
- Corporate conversions
- Hidden secured parties
- SOS indexing errors
- Failure to continue

Your defense mechanisms:

✓ Annual UCC search
✓ UCC-5 information statements
✓ Immediate refiling

CHAPTER 16

UCC Filing Audits, Maintenance & Long-Term Administrative Strategy

✓ Trust-level resolutions
✓ Updated collateral schedules

XI. Demonstrating Filing System Effectiveness (Professional Level)

To demonstrate long-term administrative effectiveness:

1. Show original UCC filings
2. Show all continuations
3. Show UCC-3 amendments
4. Show UCC-5 objections (if any)
5. Show trust resolutions
6. Show annual audit logs
7. Show calendars for future continuations
8. Show certified UCC-11 searches across multiple years

This creates an undeniable **administrative chain of custody.**

XII. Chapter Summary

Readers now understand:

✓ How to perform annual UCC audits
✓ How to track continuation cycles professionally
✓ How to monitor debtor and secured party changes
✓ How to synchronize filings across entities
✓ How to maintain a trust + LLC filing ecosystem
✓ How to detect administrative threats
✓ How to create long-term continuity
✓ How to demonstrate decades of perfection

This chapter turns a UCC filer into a **long-term secured creditor with administrative mastery**.

CHAPTER 17

Securing Intellectual Property, Digital Assets & Commercial Rights Under Article 9

Illustrated Edition — How to Collateralize, Monetize, and Protect IP Using UCC Filings

---

I. Introduction — IP Is the New Collateral

In today's economy:

- Names
- Brands
- Trademarks
- Copyrights
- Royalties
- Digital assets
- Courses
- Websites
- Social media accounts
- Content libraries

…are often **more valuable than physical assets.**

Article 9 provides a **legally recognized method** to secure and enforce rights in this property class.

II. What Types of IP Can Be Secured Under Article 9?

✓ Copyrights (registered or unregistered)

✓ Trademarks (state or federal)

✓ Personal name marks (state-regulated)

✓ Service marks

✓ Domain names & website assets

✓ Digital content libraries

✓ Royalties & revenue streams

CHAPTER 17

Securing Intellectual Property, Digital Assets & Commercial Rights Under Article 9

✓ Software, code, and databases

✓ Payment intangibles

✓ Licenses (exclusive or non-exclusive)

✓ NFTs, tokenized rights, crypto assets

Article 9 classifies these as:

- **General intangibles**
- **Payment intangibles**
- **Accounts**
- **Chattel paper** (digital or traditional)

III. What Cannot Be Secured Under Article 9

Article 9 **cannot** secure:

✗ Federal patents (require separate USPTO assignment)
✗ Federal trademarks *without assignment*
✗ Real estate title
✗ Government-issued licenses (driver's license, passport, etc.)
✗ Rights explicitly barred by statute

But:

✓ The **economic rights** of these assets
✓ Royalties
✓ Payment streams
✓ Commercial proceeds

CAN be secured under Article 9.

IV. Securing Trademarks (Including Personal Name Marks)

Trademarks fall into two categories under Article 9:

CHAPTER 17

Securing Intellectual Property, Digital Assets & Commercial Rights Under Article 9

1. State-Level Trademarks (like your Illinois mark)

✓ Fully securable
✓ Treated as general intangibles
✓ Assignable
✓ Revenue (royalties) is securable
✓ Controlled entirely by state law

2. Federal Trademarks (USPTO)

✓ Economic rights can be secured
✓ Actual trademark ownership requires a USPTO assignment
✓ The UCC filing covers revenue streams, licensing rights, and commercial use

This is an important distinction:
UCC ≠ Trademark Assignment
…but
UCC = Securing the commercial rights associated with a trademark.

V. Securing Copyrights & Creative Works

Copyrights can be secured in two ways:

1. UCC Filing (Article 9)

Secures:

✓ Royalties
✓ Licensing revenue
✓ Content libraries
✓ Economic rights
✓ Distribution rights

2. Copyright Assignment (USPTO/Library of Congress)

Transfers actual ownership.

Most creators only need Article 9 perfection unless they are selling their copyright.

CHAPTER 17

Securing Intellectual Property, Digital Assets & Commercial Rights Under Article 9

VI. Securing Digital Assets & Online Businesses

Digital assets include:

- YouTube channels
- TikTok accounts (transfer-restricted but revenue streams are securable)
- Shopify stores
- Ebook libraries
- Courses
- CRM databases
- Subscriber lists
- Software
- Digital products

What CAN be secured:

✓ Payment intangibles
✓ Accounts receivable
✓ Subscriber revenue
✓ Royalty flows
✓ Digital product rights
✓ Embedded contract rights

What CANNOT be secured directly:

✕ Platform account ownership (because ToS forbids sale/assignment)
…but the revenue can be secured.

VII. How Trusts Secure IP (Your Structure As Model)

Your trusts are perfect examples:

Secured Party:

RE 234 270 824 US Holdings
(Administrative holding trust)

Grantor / Creator:

CHAPTER 17

Securing Intellectual Property, Digital Assets & Commercial Rights Under Article 9

Rodney Cortez Carroll™

Collateral:

- Books (Paper Genocide, Born of Blood Bound by Paper)
- Trademarks (personal name mark)
- Courses
- Digital product lines
- Publishing imprint (Babylon Press)
- Royalty streams
- Brand rights

Why Trusts Are Ideal for IP:

✓ Provides generational continuity
✓ Protects commercial rights beyond creator's lifespan
✓ Allows structured licensing
✓ Makes IP monetization scalable
✓ Uses UCC to secure revenue streams

CHAPTER 17

Securing Intellectual Property, Digital Assets & Commercial Rights Under Article 9

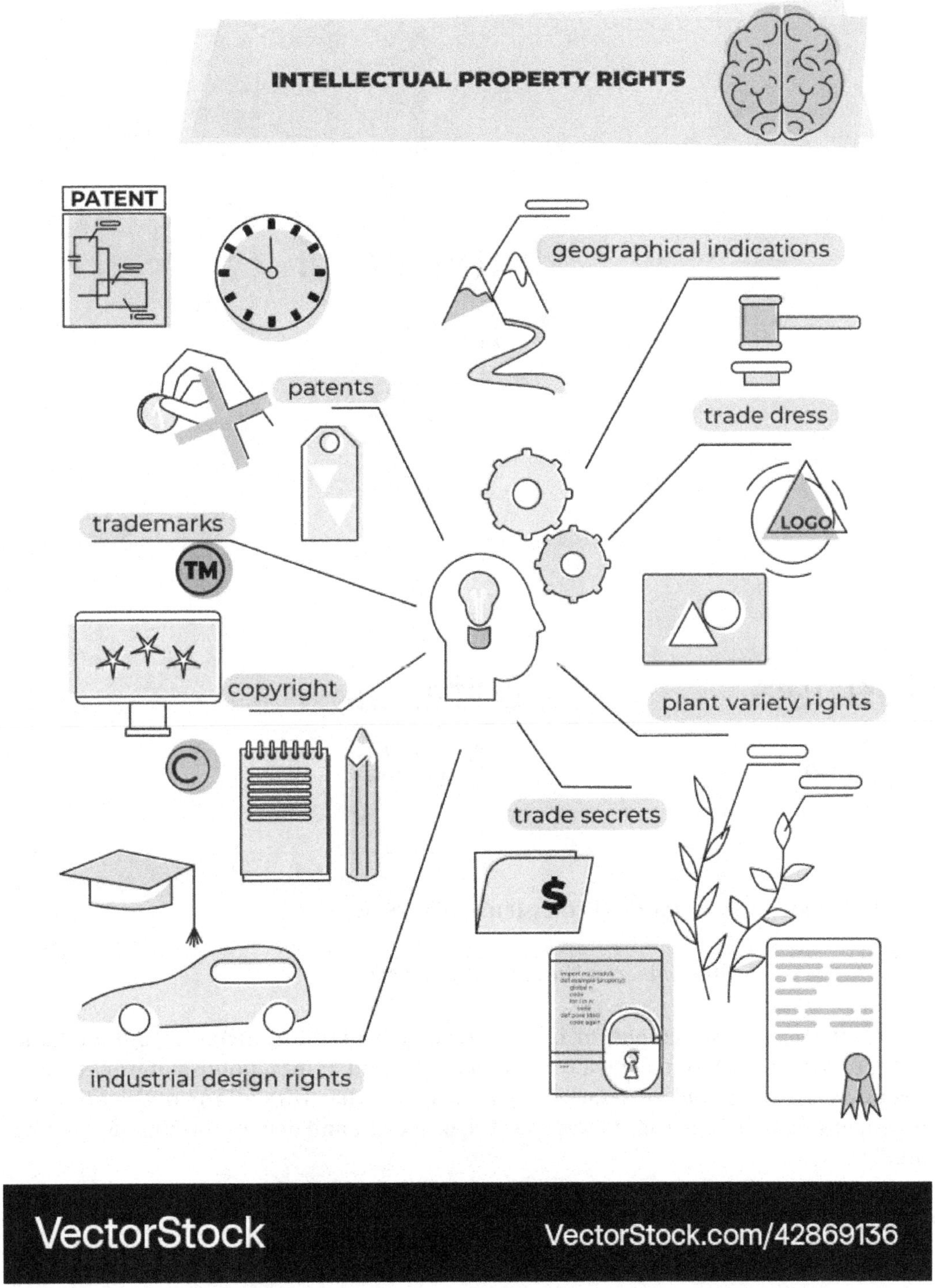

CHAPTER 17

Securing Intellectual Property, Digital Assets & Commercial Rights Under Article 9

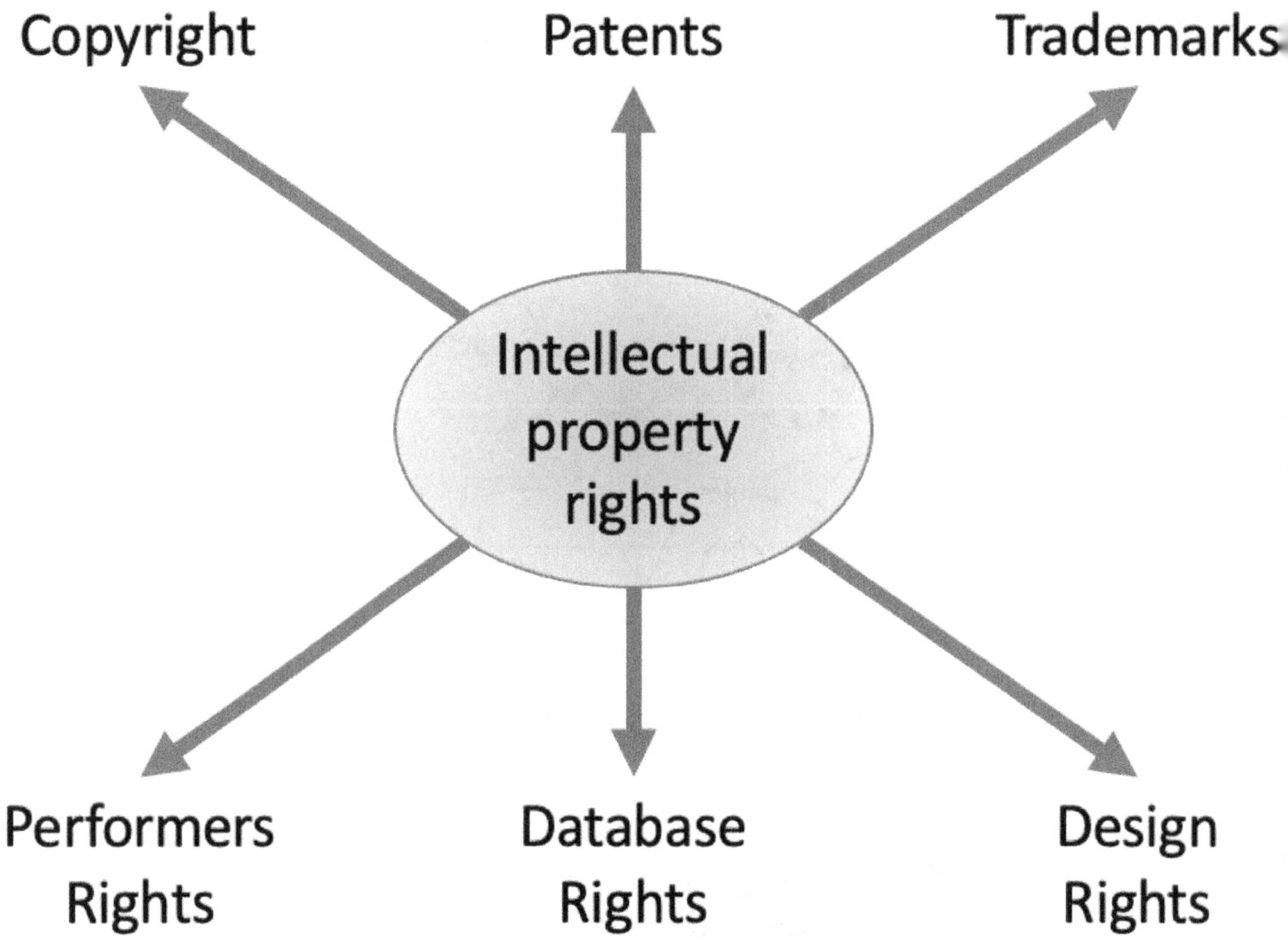

VIII. Sample Collateral Description (Professional, SOS-Safe)

Use this exact style — clean, commercial, and legally accurate.

"All intellectual property owned now or in the future by the Debtor, including but not limited to trademarks, service marks, copyrights, trade names, domain names, published works, digital content, courses, software, and all associated goodwill; together with all royalty rights, licensing rights, payment intangibles, accounts, receivables, proceeds, and general intangibles arising therefrom."

Safe, professional, and universally accepted.

CHAPTER 17

Securing Intellectual Property, Digital Assets & Commercial Rights Under Article 9

IX. Assignments of IP Rights (Using UCC-3)

UCC-3 Assignments allow:

✓ Transfer of secured rights
✓ Transfer of royalty rights
✓ Transfer of licensing rights
✓ Consolidation into a holding trust

Example:

Rodney Cortez Carroll-El Ali Living Trust
→ Assigns commercialization rights of IP
TO
RE 234 270 824 US Holdings

This produces:

- Administrative consolidation
- Priority preservation
- Estate protection
- Licensing flexibility

X. Cross-Collateralization for IP Portfolios

A single IP portfolio can secure:

✓ Loans
✓ Lines of credit
✓ Publishing advances
✓ Business operations
✓ Equipment purchases
✓ Commercial partnerships
✓ Joint ventures

A sophisticated trust-based system can:

- Consolidate all IP
- Issue licensing agreements
- Secure all revenue streams

- Maintain administrative priority

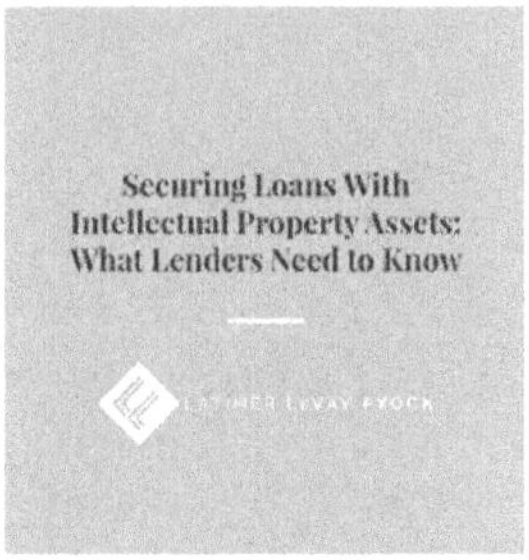

XI. Demonstrating Effectiveness of IP-Related UCC Filings

To prove a filing is valid, produce:

1. UCC-1 financing statement
2. Security agreement (for IP)
3. Copyright/trademark registrations or state filings
4. Trust or LLC resolutions
5. Royalty agreements
6. Licensing contracts
7. A certified UCC search showing active perfection

This packet makes enforcement airtight.

CHAPTER 17

Securing Intellectual Property, Digital Assets & Commercial Rights Under Article 9

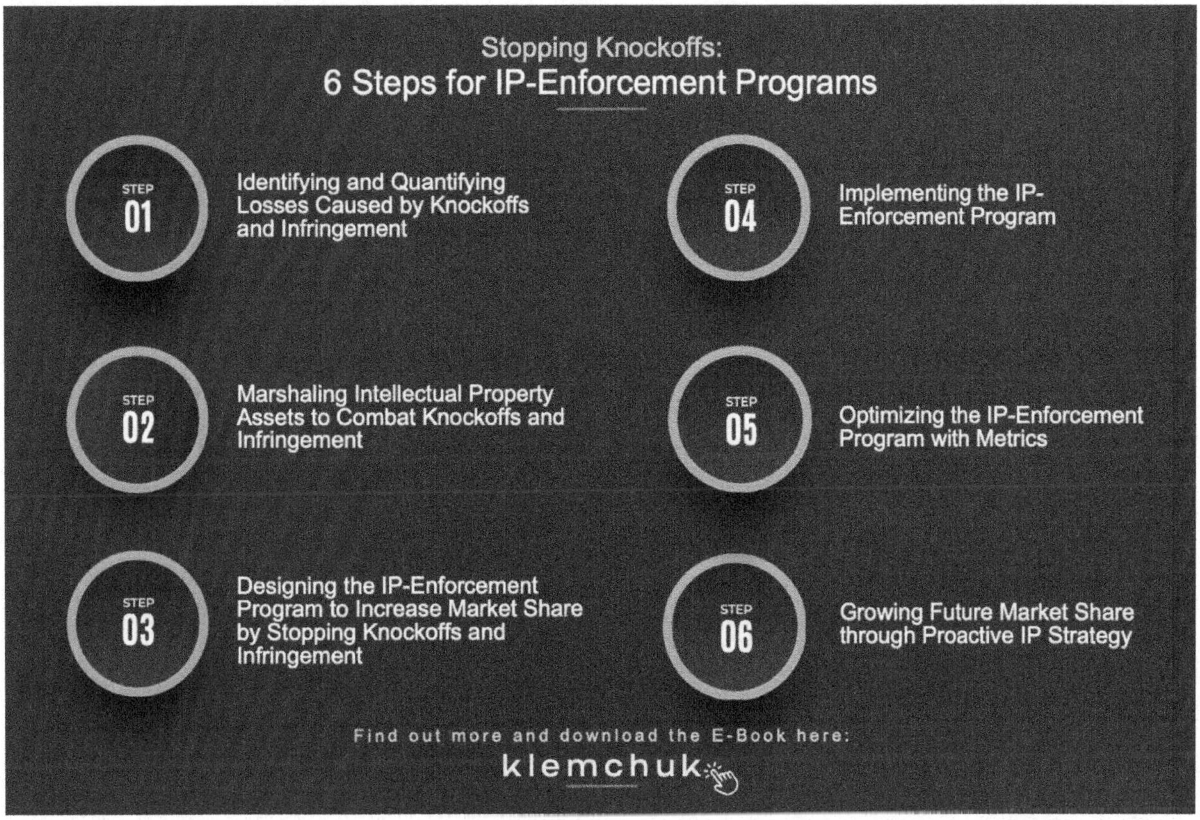

XII. Chapter Summary

Readers now understand:

✓ How IP fits into Article 9
✓ What IP assets can be secured
✓ What cannot be secured
✓ How to secure trademarks, copyrights & digital property
✓ How to use trusts for IP administration
✓ How to draft acceptable collateral descriptions
✓ How to use assignments to reorganize IP ownership
✓ How to cross-collateralize an entire IP portfolio
✓ How to create an enforcement-ready documentation chain

This chapter gives the reader the ability to treat **ideas, creativity, and brand identity** as real, bankable assets — exactly how corporations do

CHAPTER 18

Compliance, Recordkeeping & Avoiding Rejection: Ensuring Every Filing Is Accepted

The KYB

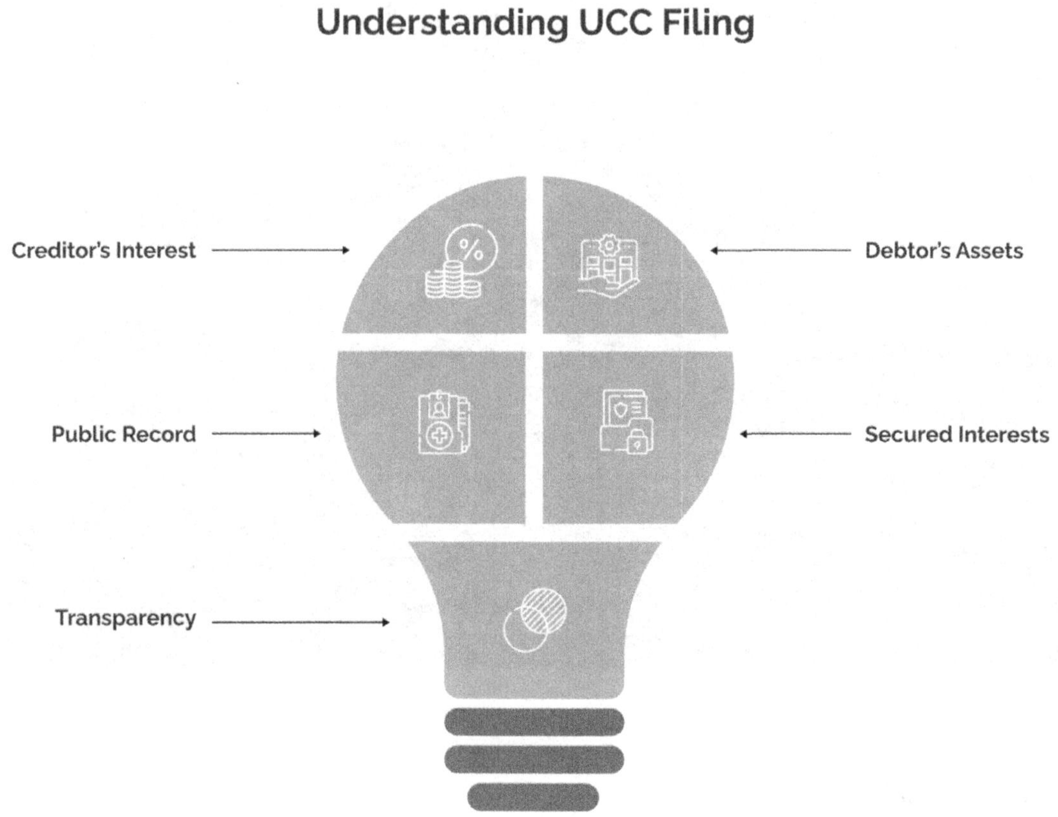

I. Introduction — Acceptance Is Everything

A UCC filing that is:

- Rejected
- Improperly indexed
- Filed in the wrong jurisdiction
- Filed with the wrong party name
- Missing required components

CHAPTER 18

Compliance, Recordkeeping & Avoiding Rejection: Ensuring Every Filing Is Accepted

…is effectively **no filing at all**.

This chapter teaches the rules banks follow to ensure **every filing is accepted on the first attempt**.

II. The Four Core Compliance Pillars

Every effective and accepted UCC filing must satisfy:

✓ **Pillar 1 — Correct Debtor Name**

✓ **Pillar 2 — Correct Secured Party Name**

✓ **Pillar 3 — Acceptable Collateral Description**

✓ **Pillar 4 — Correct Filing Location**

If any of these four are wrong → the entire filing fails.

III. Core Compliance Pillar #1 — Correct Debtor Name (MOST IMPORTANT)

Errors in debtor names cause **80%+ of all UCC rejections**.

For Individuals:

✓ Use the exact name on government ID
✓ No nicknames
✓ No abbreviations
✓ No extra punctuation
✓ No trust designators if filing against a person

For LLCs, Corporations, and Organizations:

✓ Use the name exactly as shown on the Articles of Organization/Formation
✓ Match capitalization
✓ Include commas, periods, and spacing
✓ Include corporate endings ("LLC," "Inc.," "Corp.")

For Trusts:

File against the **trust name**, NOT the trustee personally.

Format:

CHAPTER 18

Compliance, Recordkeeping & Avoiding Rejection: Ensuring Every Filing Is Accepted

[Trust Name]
c/o **[Trustee Name], Trustee**
[Address]

IV. Core Compliance Pillar #2 — Correct Secured Party Name

A secured party's name must also be:

- Exact
- Complete
- Identical to legal documents
- Not abbreviated

When the secured party is a trust, include:

✓ Trust name
✓ Trustee name
✓ Trustee title ("Trustee")

Example:

RE 234 270 824 US Holdings
c/o Rodney Cortez Carroll™, Trustee

V. Core Compliance Pillar #3 — Acceptable Collateral Description

An acceptable collateral description must be:

✓ Clear
✓ Commercially recognizable
✓ Not misleading
✓ Not philosophical
✓ Not jurisdictional in nature

Examples of **good** descriptions:

- "All business equipment and inventory owned or hereafter acquired."
- "All accounts, payment intangibles, and proceeds thereof."
- "All intellectual property including trademarks, copyrights, and associated royalties."

CHAPTER 18

Compliance, Recordkeeping & Avoiding Rejection: Ensuring Every Filing Is Accepted

Examples of **bad** descriptions:

❌ "My flesh and blood"
❌ "My sovereignty"
❌ "All real property in the United States"
❌ "My trust estate in its entirety"
❌ "All rights known and unknown in the universe"

Below is the visual.

Image: Acceptable vs. Unacceptable Collateral Descriptions

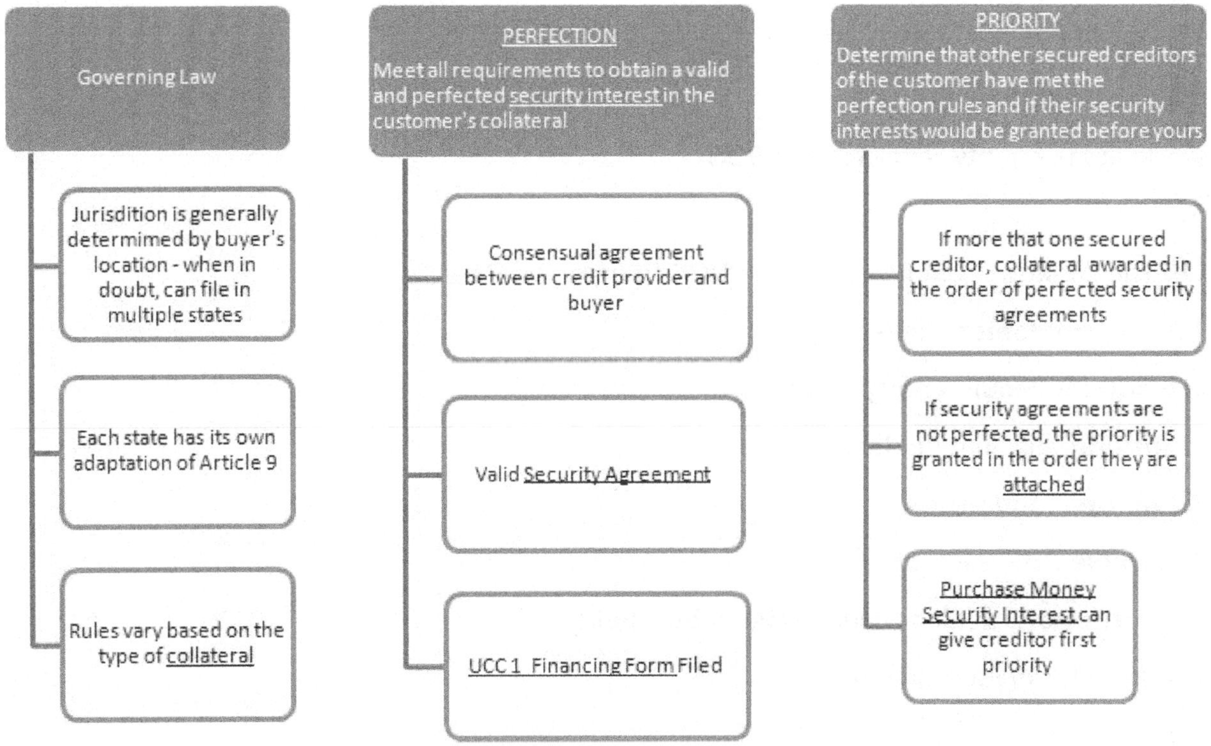

VI. Core Compliance Pillar #4 — Correct Filing Location

Filing in the wrong place results in:

- The filing being legally ineffective
- Loss of priority

CHAPTER 18

Compliance, Recordkeeping & Avoiding Rejection: Ensuring Every Filing Is Accepted

- Rejection or mis-indexing

Standard Rule:

✓ File in the **state of the debtor's location**

For organizations:

✓ State of formation

For individuals:

✓ State of principal residence

For trusts:

✓ State where trust is administered

Fixture filings:

✓ File at the **county recorder**, not SOS

VII. The 20 Most Common Reasons UCC Filings Are Rejected

1. Incorrect debtor name

2. Incorrect secured party name

3. Missing required fields

4. Improper addresses

5. Illegible PDF uploads

6. Overuse of trust language in the debtor field

7. Wrong filing jurisdiction

8. Filing real property claims

9. Filing sovereign or metaphysical language

10. Missing filing fee

11. Collateral description too vague

12. Collateral description too philosophical

13. Unauthorized filer

CHAPTER 18

Compliance, Recordkeeping & Avoiding Rejection: Ensuring Every Filing Is Accepted

14. Filing against a non-existent entity

15. Filing into a dissolved entity

16. Listing a human being as collateral

17. Wrong indexing data

18. Attempting to lien government property

19. Attempting to lien land

20. Submitting a continuation too early or too late

VIII. Recordkeeping Requirements for Professional Filers

A professional UCC system includes:

✓ **Trust minutes**

✓ **Resolutions**

✓ **Collateral schedules**

✓ **Ledger entries**

✓ **Digital and physical copies of all filings**

✓ **Administrative calendar**

✓ **UCC-11 searches annually**

✓ **Backup storage**

IX. SOS Portal Formatting Rules (Universal Principles)

Although each state varies, universal formatting rules include:

✓ No bold claims
✓ No metaphysics
✓ No references to federal supremacy
✓ No "all rights reserved" clauses
✓ No excessive punctuation

CHAPTER 18

Compliance, Recordkeeping & Avoiding Rejection: Ensuring Every Filing Is Accepted

✓ Fit collateral description in the allowed field if possible
✓ Use attachments only when necessary

X. Trust-Specific Compliance (Your System Modeled)

Trust filings must include:

✓ Trust name
✓ Trustee name
✓ Trustee authority (resolution or certificate)
✓ Trust jurisdiction
✓ Correct debtor type

Your structure is the **gold standard** example:

Secured Party:
RE 234 270 824 US Holdings
c/o Rodney Cortez Carroll™, Trustee

Debtor:
Babylon Industries LLC
or
Rodney Cortez Carroll-El Ali Living Trust

XI. Maintaining an Error-Free System — Annual Checklist

Each year:

1. Verify debtor names
2. Verify secured party names
3. Update trust resolutions
4. Confirm collateral schedules
5. Run a UCC-11 search
6. Prepare continuation reminders
7. Reconcile trust and LLC records
8. Archive filings in multiple formats

Below is the visual.

CHAPTER 18

Compliance, Recordkeeping & Avoiding Rejection: Ensuring Every Filing Is Accepted

---

Image: Annual UCC System Maintenance Checklist

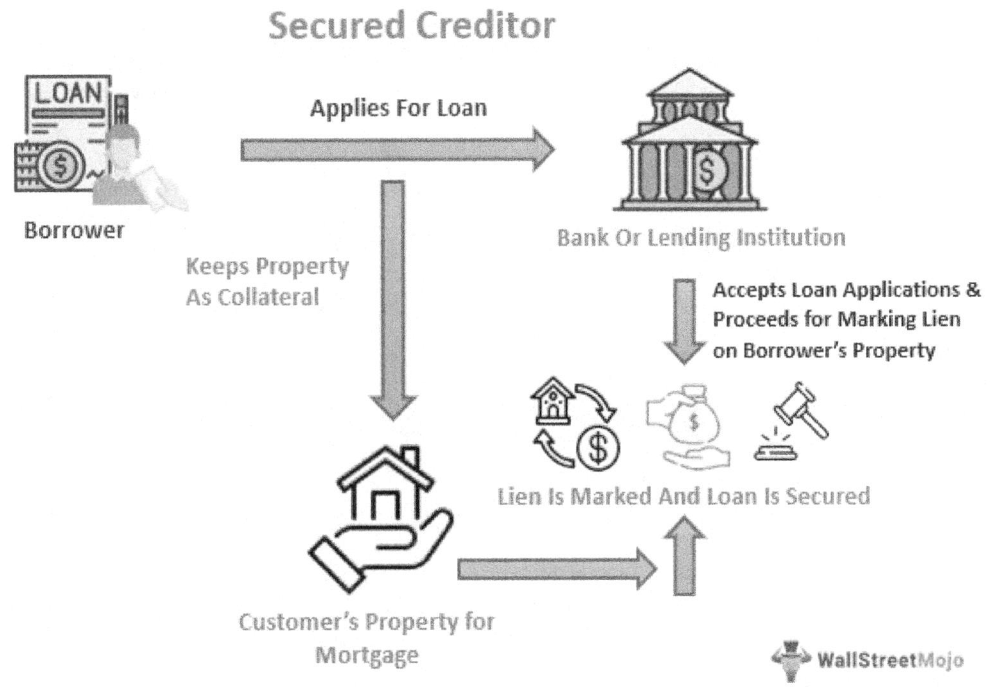

CHAPTER 18

Compliance, Recordkeeping & Avoiding Rejection: Ensuring Every Filing Is Accepted

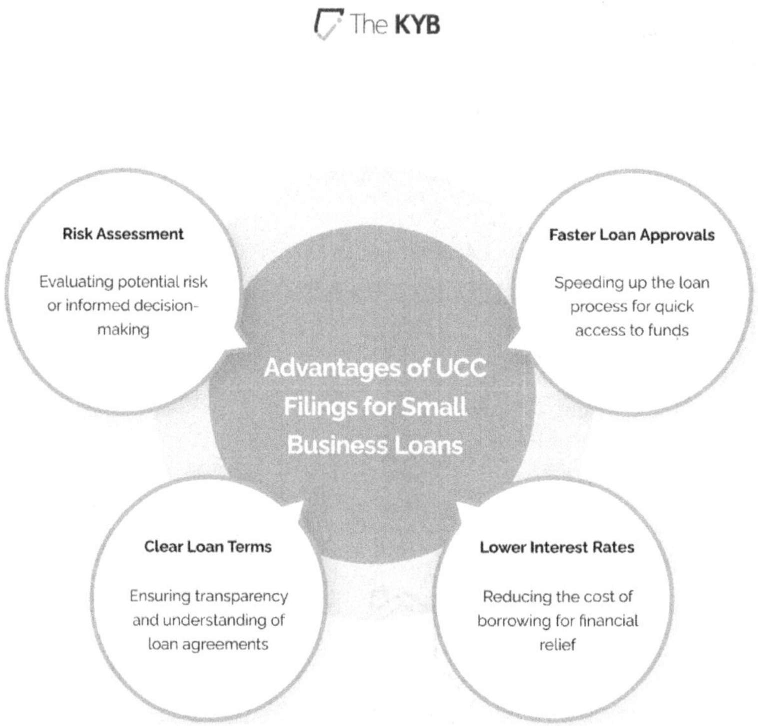

XII. Demonstrating Compliance to Courts, Lenders, or Agencies

To prove your filing system is compliant:

✓ Produce UCC-1
✓ Produce security agreement
✓ Produce trust resolutions
✓ Produce UCC-3 amendments
✓ Produce continuation filings
✓ Produce certified UCC-11 search
✓ Produce your Master Filing Log
✓ Produce collateral schedules

This demonstrates:

- Professional administration

CHAPTER 18

Compliance, Recordkeeping & Avoiding Rejection: Ensuring Every Filing Is Accepted

- Due diligence
- Clean priority
- Lawful authority

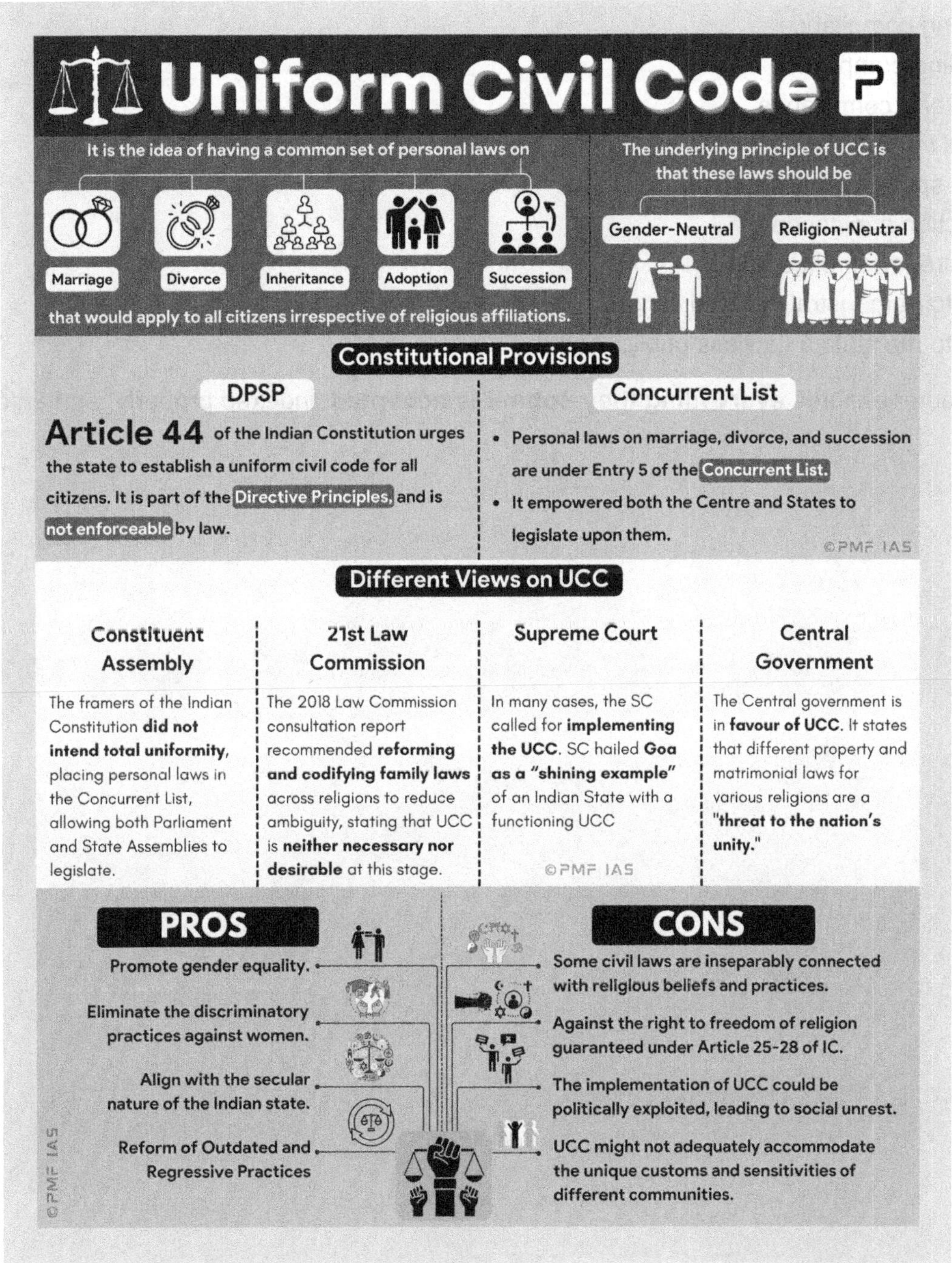

CHAPTER 18

Compliance, Recordkeeping & Avoiding Rejection: Ensuring Every Filing Is Accepted

XIII. Chapter Summary

Readers now understand:

✓ Naming compliance
✓ Location compliance
✓ Collateral compliance
✓ Portal formatting rules
✓ Trust-specific considerations
✓ Rejection avoidance
✓ Required recordkeeping
✓ How to demonstrate a valid filing
✓ How to maintain a flawless public record

This chapter ensures **every filing they submit is accepted**, indexed properly, and enforceable.

CHAPTER 19

Multi-State Filing Strategies, Jurisdiction & Debtor Location Rules

I. Introduction — UCC Jurisdiction Is About LOCATION, Not Property

Most people mistakenly believe:

- You file where the collateral is
- You file where the secured party lives
- You file where the contract was signed

None of this is accurate.

Under Article 9, **you file where the DEBTOR is located**.

Everything — *priority, perfection, enforceability* — is tied to the **debtor's jurisdiction**.

UCC FINANCING STATEMENT
FOLLOW INSTRUCTIONS
A. NAME & PHONE OF CONTACT AT FILER (optional)
B. E-MAIL CONTACT AT FILER (optional)
C. SEND ACKNOWLEDGMENT TO: (Name and Address)

Print Reset

THE ABOVE SPACE IS FOR FILING OFFICE USE ONLY

1. DEBTOR'S NAME: Provide only one Debtor name (1a or 1b) (use exact, full name; do not omit, modify, or abbreviate any part of the Debtor's name); if any part of the Individual Debtor's name will not fit in line 1b, leave all of item 1 blank, check here ☐ and provide the Individual Debtor information in item 10 of the Financing Statement Addendum (Form UCC1Ad)

1a. ORGANIZATION'S NAME
OR
1b. INDIVIDUAL'S SURNAME | FIRST PERSONAL NAME | ADDITIONAL NAME(S)/INITIAL(S) | SUFFIX
1c. MAILING ADDRESS | CITY | STATE | POSTAL CODE | COUNTRY

2. DEBTOR'S NAME: Provide only one Debtor name (2a or 2b) (use exact, full name; do not omit, modify, or abbreviate any part of the Debtor's name); if any part of the Individual Debtor's name will not fit in line 2b, leave all of item 2 blank, check here ☐ and provide the Individual Debtor information in item 10 of the Financing Statement Addendum (Form UCC1Ad)

2a. ORGANIZATION'S NAME
OR
2b. INDIVIDUAL'S SURNAME | FIRST PERSONAL NAME | ADDITIONAL NAME(S)/INITIAL(S) | SUFFIX
2c. MAILING ADDRESS | CITY | STATE | POSTAL CODE | COUNTRY

3. SECURED PARTY'S NAME (or NAME of ASSIGNEE of ASSIGNOR SECURED PARTY): Provide only one Secured Party name (3a or 3b)

3a. ORGANIZATION'S NAME
OR
3b. INDIVIDUAL'S SURNAME | FIRST PERSONAL NAME | ADDITIONAL NAME(S)/INITIAL(S) | SUFFIX
3c. MAILING ADDRESS | CITY | STATE | POSTAL CODE | COUNTRY

4. COLLATERAL: This financing statement covers the following collateral:

II. How Article 9 Defines "Debtor Location"

CHAPTER 19

Multi-State Filing Strategies, Jurisdiction & Debtor Location Rules

✓ **If the debtor is an individual:**

Location = **State of principal residence**

✓ **If the debtor is an LLC or corporation:**

Location = **State of organization**

✓ **If the debtor is a trust:**

Location = **State where the trust is administered**
(Usually listed in the trust declaration)

✓ **If the debtor is a foreign entity (non-U.S.):**

Location =

- The jurisdiction whose law governs the entity **OR**
- **Washington, D.C.**, if the governing jurisdiction has no UCC-type filing system

---

III. Why Collateral Location Usually Does NOT Matter

The UCC filing system focuses on personal property **rights**, not physical location.

Therefore:

✓ A car in Georgia
✓ Equipment in Texas
✓ Accounts receivable in Illinois
✓ IP rights nationwide

...all require filing **in the debtor's home jurisdiction**, not the collateral location.

Narrow Exception: Fixture Filings

Fixture filings **must be recorded in the county where the property is located** (covered in Chapter 15).

IV. Multi-State Business Operations — How to File Correctly

A business may:

- Operate in multiple states
- Own assets in multiple states

CHAPTER 19

Multi-State Filing Strategies, Jurisdiction & Debtor Location Rules

- Have offices nationwide

But:

You still file ONLY in the state where the entity was formed.

Examples:

Entity	**Operates In**	**State of Formation**	**Filing Location**
Babylon Industries LLC	IL, IN, OH	Illinois	Illinois SOS
A Nevada LLC operating in 10 states	10 states	Nevada	Nevada SOS
Texas corporation with land in Missouri	Missouri	Texas	Texas SOS

V. When You MUST File in More Than One State

There are **three situations** where multi-state filings are necessary:

---

1. COLLATERAL THAT MOVES (e.g., transportation fleets)

If the debtor is located in State A, file in State A.
If vehicles are titled in other states, **note the secured party on each title**.

---

2. FIXTURE FILINGS

Fixture filing → County land records
General filing → State SOS

---

3. PROPERTY LOCATED OUTSIDE THE U.S.

Assets in a foreign country may require:

- A UCC filing in debtor's state
- A local filing under foreign property law

VI. Trusts Operating in Multiple States

CHAPTER 19

Multi-State Filing Strategies, Jurisdiction & Debtor Location Rules

A trust may own:

- Property in several states
- LLCs in multiple states
- Trademarks, royalties, digital assets nationwide

But UCC filings always depend on:

✓ The trust's administrative home

—not the trustee's residence
—not the property location

For example:

RE 234 270 824 US Holdings
→ If administered in Illinois
→ All UCC filings "located" in Illinois

Even if the trust owns assets in:

- Florida
- Arizona
- California
- Mexico
- Overseas

CHAPTER 19

Multi-State Filing Strategies, Jurisdiction & Debtor Location Rules

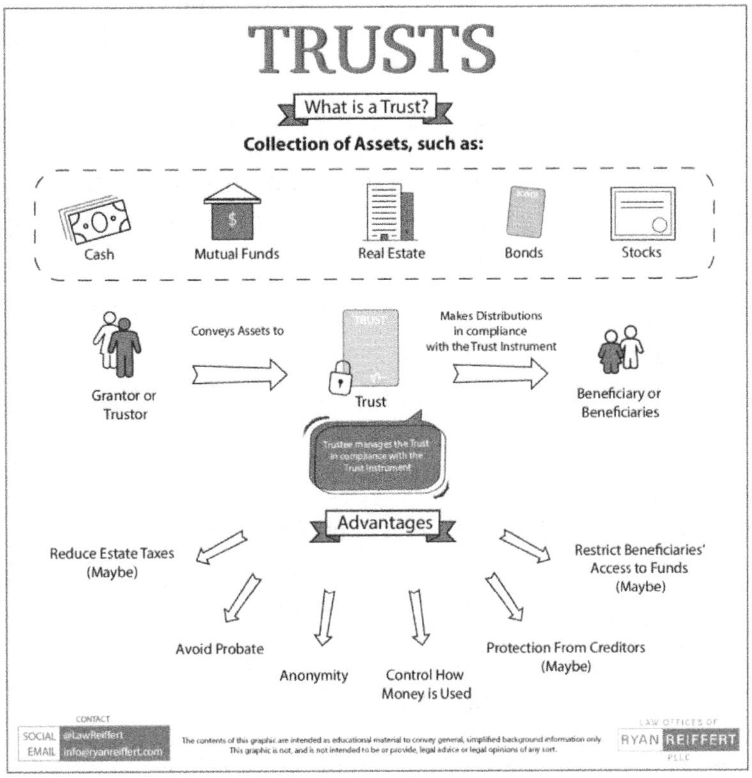

VII. Foreign Debtors & International Assets

If the debtor is formed **outside the United States**, Article 9 applies only if:

- The entity's home jurisdiction does NOT have a UCC-equivalent
- In such cases → File in **Washington, D.C.**

Examples:

Foreign Entity	Home Law?	Filing Location
Canadian corporation	Yes	Canada (domestic law)
Belize trust	No UCC-like system	Washington, D.C.
Cayman LLC	Yes	Cayman government
Mexican business	Yes	Mexico

CHAPTER 19

Multi-State Filing Strategies, Jurisdiction & Debtor Location Rules

VIII. Changing Debtor Location — What Happens to Perfection?

If a debtor relocates to another state:

✓ Perfection continues TEMPORARILY (usually 4 months)

✓ After 4 months → Filing becomes ineffective unless re-filed in the new state

This rule prevents:

- Gamesmanship
- Relocation to escape UCC liens
- Administrative loopholes

IX. Multi-State Enforcement — Which State's Law Applies?

If enforcement occurs:

- **Perfection** follows debtor location
- **Priority** follows first jurisdiction of filing
- **Repossession** follows the law where collateral is located
- **Contracts** follow choice-of-law clause
- **Disputes** may involve multiple courts

X. Special Case — Multi-State Intellectual Property

IP is inherently borderless.

But UCC jurisdiction still depends on:

✓ Where the debtor is located

NOT where the IP is used
NOT where royalties are generated
NOT where customers are located

Example:

Babylon Press sells books globally.
Royalties flow from multiple nations.
But:

CHAPTER 19

Multi-State Filing Strategies, Jurisdiction & Debtor Location Rules

Filings still occur in the debtor's location only.

XI. Demonstrating Effectiveness in Multi-State Systems

To prove your filing is correct across state lines:

Produce:

1. Original UCC-1
2. All amendments
3. Trust or LLC resolutions
4. Choice-of-law clause in the security agreement
5. Certified UCC search from correct jurisdiction
6. Evidence of debtor location
7. Filing in county land records (if fixtures)
8. Filing in foreign jurisdiction (if required)

Courts want a **complete jurisdictional chain**, not scattered filings.

XII. Chapter Summary

Readers now understand:

✓ How debtor location controls filing jurisdiction
✓ Why collateral location rarely matters
✓ When multi-state filings *are* required
✓ How trusts operating across states must file
✓ How foreign entities are handled
✓ The 4-month relocation rule
✓ Multi-state enforcement laws
✓ How IP and digital businesses work in multi-state systems
✓ How to prove a multi-state UCC filing is valid

This chapter makes the entire manual **interstate- and international-ready**, elevating it to a true professional reference.

CHAPTER 20

Enforcement, Litigation Strategy & Practical Application of UCC Rights in Real Disputes

I. Introduction — The UCC Is a Framework, Not a Weapon

The most important truth:

A UCC filing does not force anything.
A UCC filing *positions* you to win.

Article 9 gives secured parties:

✓ Priority
✓ Standing
✓ Collection rights
✓ Enforcement pathways
✓ Leverage in negotiation

But the **real power** comes from:

- Documentation
- Precision
- Consistency
- Administrative clarity
- Demonstrated value

II. The Enforcement Pyramid — Three Layers of Power

There are **three levels** of enforcement power:

Layer 1 — Administrative Power (Private Documents)

✓ Security agreements
✓ Trust resolutions
✓ Ledgers
✓ Minutes
✓ Notices

Layer 2 — Public Power (UCC Filings)

✓ UCC-1
✓ UCC-3
✓ Continuations
✓ UCC-5 objections

CHAPTER 20

Enforcement, Litigation Strategy & Practical Application of UCC Rights in Real Disputes

Layer 3 — Judicial Power (Courts)

✓ Enforcement lawsuits
✓ Repossession orders
✓ Garnishments
✓ Bankruptcy priority

III. How Courts Evaluate UCC-Based Claims

Courts look for **five things only**:

✓ 1. A valid security agreement

✓ 2. A valid UCC-1 filing

✓ 3. A clear collateral description

✓ 4. Evidence of value given

✓ 5. A default by the debtor

If these five points are proven, enforcement is nearly automatic.

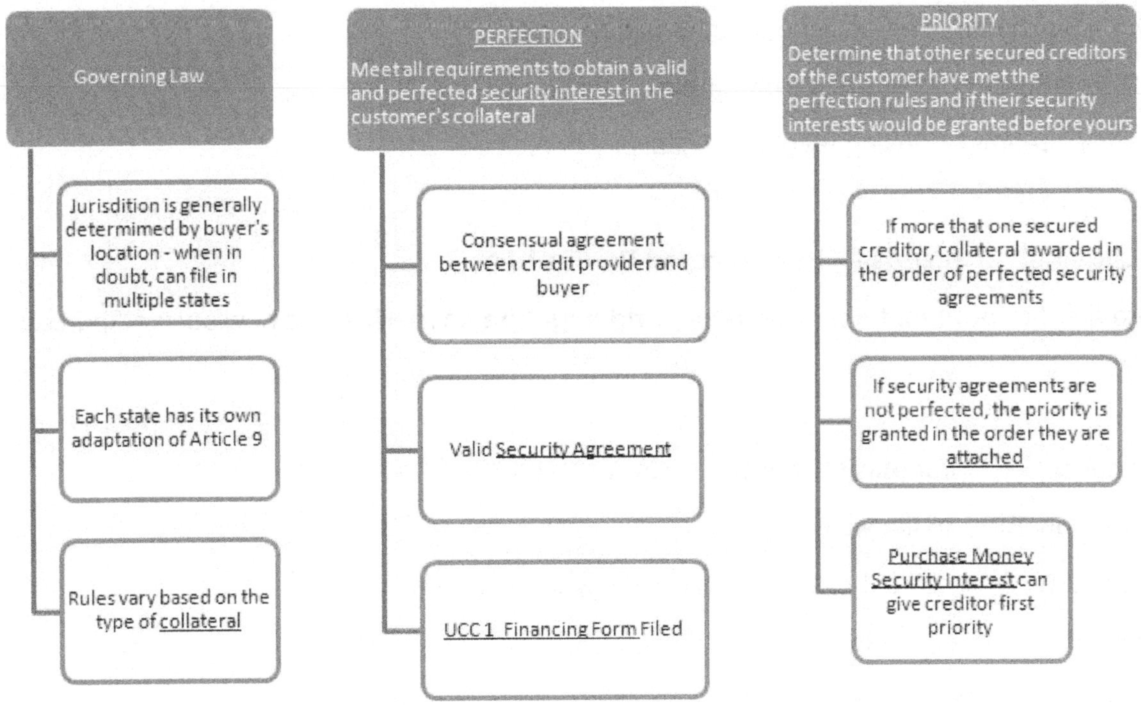

CHAPTER 20

Enforcement, Litigation Strategy & Practical Application of UCC Rights in Real Disputes

IV. Enforcement Tools Secured Parties Actually Use

When a debtor defaults, the secured party has several lawful tools:

---

1. Demand for Payment (Formal Default Notice)

Triggers the enforcement process.

2. Notice to Account Debtors

Debtor's customers now pay YOU instead of them.

3. Self-Help Repossession (if peaceful & authorized)

Machinery, equipment, vehicles, tools, etc.

4. Judicial Action

Secured parties can file suit to enforce rights.

5. Commercially Reasonable Sale

Sell collateral to satisfy the debt.

6. Setoff and Recoupment

If you owe the debtor money under other agreements.

7. Garnishment of Payment Intangibles

Royalty streams, licensing revenue, digital payments.

V. Litigation Scenarios — How Secured Parties Win

Here are the **four most common real-world litigation scenarios** and how secured parties prevail:

Scenario 1 — Competing Creditors (Priority Battle)

Resolution: **First to file wins**.

If your UCC-1 predates theirs, you win nearly every time.

Scenario 2 — Debtor Bankruptcy

CHAPTER 20

Enforcement, Litigation Strategy & Practical Application of UCC Rights in Real Disputes

Your status becomes:

✓ **"Perfected Secured Creditor"**

This is one of the strongest possible positions.
You are paid before most other creditors.

Scenario 3 — Default on a Secured Loan

Court orders:

✓ Turnover of collateral
✓ Payment of proceeds
✓ Sale of encumbered assets

Scenario 4 — Unauthorized Termination or Fraudulent Filing

Court evaluates:

✓ Your original filing
✓ Evidence of authority
✓ Administrative chain
✓ Whether termination was valid

Strong documentation = guaranteed reinstatement.

CHAPTER 20

Enforcement, Litigation Strategy & Practical Application of UCC Rights in Real Disputes

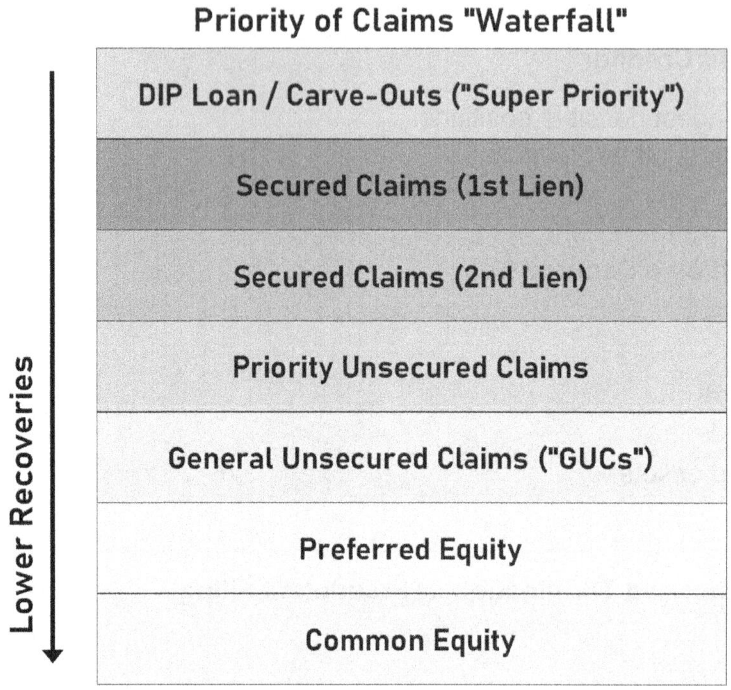

VI. Enforcement Strategy for Trust-Based Creditors (YOUR SYSTEM)

Your ecosystem is a model for advanced enforcement:

Secured Party:

RE 234 270 824 US Holdings
(Administrative holding trust)

Secondary Secured Party / Operating Trust:

Rodney Cortez Carroll-El Ali Living Trust

Debtor:

Babylon Industries LLC
(or individuals in private arrangements)

Enforcement Steps Your System Would Use:

1. Administrative demand

CHAPTER 20

Enforcement, Litigation Strategy & Practical Application of UCC Rights in Real Disputes

2. Trust resolution authorizing enforcement
3. Notice to account debtors
4. Collateral control (Article 9 self-help)
5. Litigation (if required)
6. Bankruptcy priority assertion
7. Commercially reasonable sale

CHAPTER 20

Enforcement, Litigation Strategy & Practical Application of UCC Rights in Real Disputes

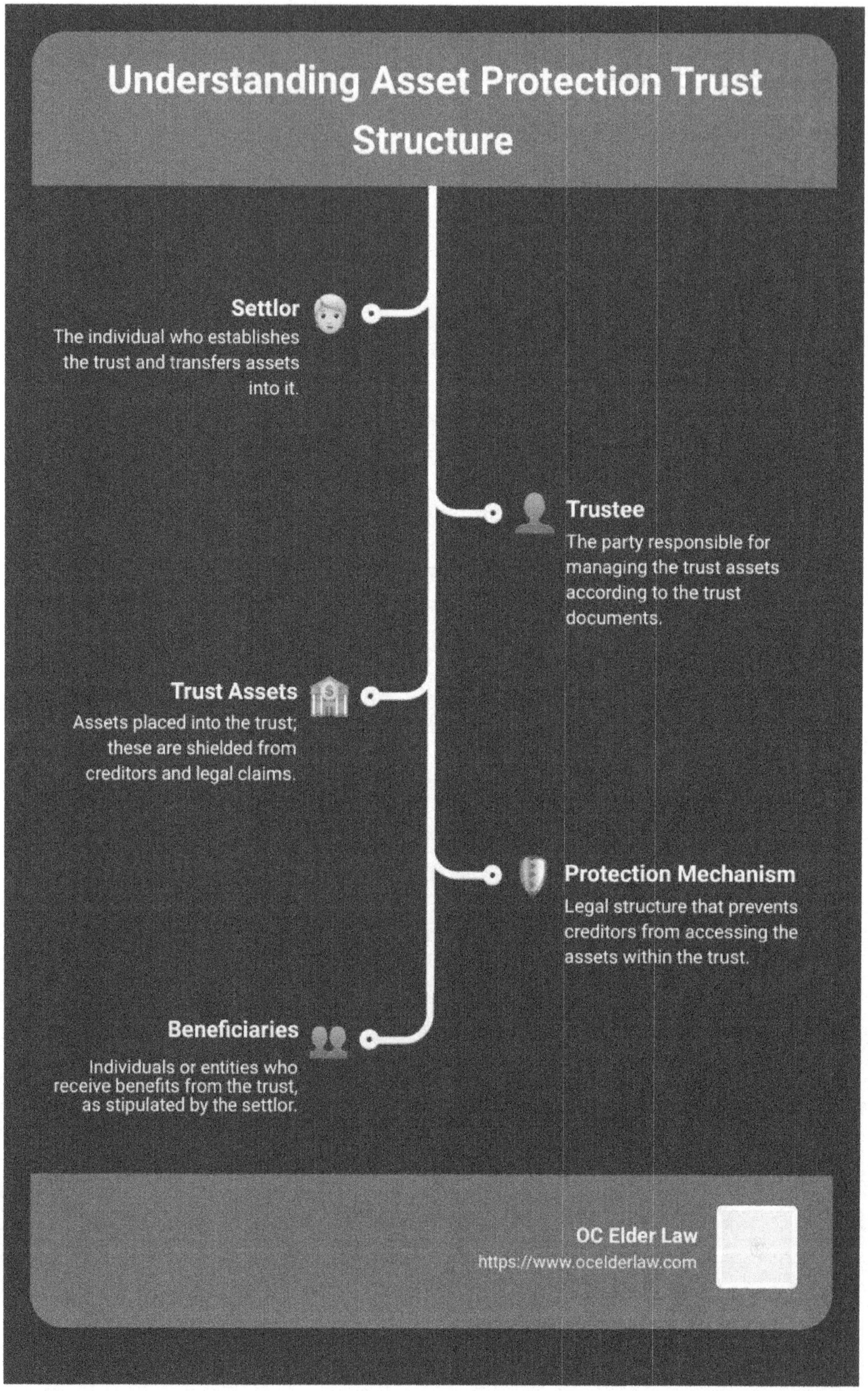

CHAPTER 20

Enforcement, Litigation Strategy & Practical Application of UCC Rights in Real Disputes

VII. Negotiation Strategy — The Real Power of Article 9

Most cases never reach court because **secured parties negotiate from a position of power.**

✓ **"You cannot transfer or sell this asset without satisfying my interest."**

✓ **"I have priority over all your other creditors."**

✓ **"Your customers legally owe me, not you."**

✓ **"My trust holds perfected secured rights."**

✓ **"I can repossess and liquidate collateral if we don't settle."**

Perfected security interests change the tone of negotiations immediately.

VIII. The Enforcement Dossier — Your Winning Package

Every strong secured party maintains an enforcement dossier that contains:

✓ **1. Executed Security Agreement**

✓ **2. UCC-1 Filing**

✓ **3. UCC-3 Amendments**

✓ **4. Trust Resolutions**

✓ **5. Collateral Schedules**

✓ **6. Ledger Entries (Value Given)**

✓ **7. Notices to Debtor**

✓ **8. Certified UCC-11 Searches**

✓ **9. Payment history**

✓ **10. Default correspondence**

When presented to:

- A court
- A debtor
- A bankruptcy trustee

- Another creditor

…this dossier is **devastatingly effective**.

IX. Real Dispute Examples (Simplified)

Example 1 — Business Equipment Loan Default

Outcome: Secured party repossesses machinery, sells it, and applies proceeds to debt.

Example 2 — Competing Creditors on Inventory Financing

Outcome: Earlier filer wins priority → second creditor gets nothing from liquidation.

Example 3 — Trust Enforcing Royalty Interests

Outcome: Court orders debtor to redirect all royalty payments to the trust.

Example 4 — Debtor Bankruptcy

Outcome: Secured party receives payment before taxes, contractors, employees, or unsecured creditors.

X. When Enforcement Fails — And Why

Enforcement generally fails only when:

❌ Collateral description was defective
❌ Debtor name was incorrect
❌ Filing was in the wrong jurisdiction
❌ No underlying security agreement existed
❌ Filing lapsed (continuation missed)
❌ Trust records were incomplete

This chapter ties back to Chapters 1–19:
Correct filings + correct administration = unstoppable enforcement.

XI. Secured Party vs. Unsecured Party — Practical Difference

CHAPTER 20

Enforcement, Litigation Strategy & Practical Application of UCC Rights in Real Disputes

Issue	**Unsecured Party**	**Secured Party**
Bankruptcy	At the bottom	Near the top
Default	Must sue first	May repossess or notify
Collateral	None	Full interest
Priority	Low	Highest
Negotiation	Weak	Very strong
Recovery	Often zero	Typically high

XII. Chapter Summary — The Power of Positioning

Readers now understand:

✓ How to enforce under Article 9
✓ What courts require
✓ How to assemble a winning enforcement dossier
✓ How secured parties dominate negotiations
✓ How bankruptcy priority works
✓ How trusts enforce rights
✓ How to handle litigation
✓ How multi-state enforcement functions
✓ Why precision filing = unstoppable leverage

This is the final professional layer of your guidebook.

GLOSSARY OF UCC TERMS

Essential Article 9 Definitions for Practical Use

Account
A right to payment for goods sold or services rendered. Includes receivables.

Account Debtor
A person or business responsible for paying a debt covered by a secured interest.

After-Acquired Property
Collateral obtained by the debtor after the security agreement is executed.

Assignment (UCC-3)
A filing that transfers secured party rights to another party.

Attachment
The moment a security interest becomes enforceable against a debtor.

Bankruptcy Priority
The order in which creditors are paid in bankruptcy; perfected secured creditors are near the top.

Buyer in Ordinary Course
A purchaser who buys goods in good faith; may take goods free of some security interests.

Chattel Paper
A record or records that evidence both a monetary obligation and a security interest in goods.

Collateral
Property subject to a security interest.

Continuation (UCC-3)
Extends a UCC-1 filing for an additional five years.

Control
A method of perfecting certain collateral types (deposit accounts, investment property).

Debtor
The person or entity whose collateral is subject to the security interest.

Default
Violation of the agreement; triggers enforcement rights.

Deposit Account
A bank account used as collateral; requires "control" to perfect.

Equipment
Goods used primarily in business operations.

Financing Statement (UCC-1)
Public notice of a secured party's claim against collateral.

Fixture Filing
A UCC filing in county land records for items attached to real estate.

GLOSSARY OF UCC TERMS

General Intangibles
A category including intellectual property, payment rights, and more.

Good Faith Purchaser
A buyer who purchases collateral without knowledge of a competing security interest.

Lien Creditor
A creditor who has obtained a judgment or legal lien.

Perfection
The act of making a security interest publicly enforceable against third parties.

PMSI (Purchase-Money Security Interest)
A special type of security interest with enhanced priority for helping a debtor acquire goods.

Priority
Determines which secured party gets paid first when collateral is liquidated.

Proceeds
Whatever is received upon the sale, exchange, or disposition of collateral.

Security Agreement
The private contract creating the security interest.

Secured Party
The entity claiming an interest in debtor's collateral.

Termination (UCC-3)
Releases the secured party's interest; must be authorized.

Unperfected Interest
A security interest that is enforceable against the debtor but not against third parties.

FULL UCC FILING CHECKLIST SYSTEM

For UCC-1, UCC-3, Amendments & Enforcement Readiness

✓ UCC-1 Filing Checklist

Before Drafting

□ Confirm debtor's exact legal name
□ Confirm secured party's exact legal name
□ Gather full addresses for both parties
□ Confirm correct filing jurisdiction
□ Draft or confirm existing security agreement

Drafting the Filing

□ Enter debtor name exactly as in SOS records (business) or ID (individual)
□ Enter secured party name exactly as legally defined
□ Use acceptable collateral description
□ Avoid prohibited language (philosophical, metaphysical, jurisdictional)
□ Ensure description matches the security agreement

Before Submitting

□ Review spelling, punctuation, formatting
□ Confirm payment method
□ Attach supporting schedules only if necessary
□ Verify PDF attachments are legible

After Filing

□ Save acknowledgment receipt
□ Save filing number
□ Insert into trust/LLC administrative binder
□ Update continuation reminder (5-year calendar)

✓ UCC-3 Amendment Checklist

Determine the Amendment Type

□ Assignment
□ Continuation
□ Termination
□ Collateral amendment
□ Party information amendment

Drafting

□ Reference original UCC-1 file number
□ Accurately indicate amendment purpose
□ Confirm authority to amend (trust resolution or contract)

FULL UCC FILING CHECKLIST SYSTEM

After Filing

□ Save acknowledgment
□ Update administrative records
□ Update continuation calendar if applicable

✓ Enforcement-Ready Documentation Checklist

To prepare an **enforcement dossier**, gather:

□ Executed security agreement
□ UCC-1 financing statement
□ UCC-3 amendment filings
□ Trust resolutions or corporate authorizations
□ Ledger entries proving value given
□ Collateral schedules
□ Default notice
□ Proof of delivery of notices
□ Certified UCC-11 search results
□ Internal minutes or administrative updates

✓ Annual UCC System Maintenance Checklist

□ Verify debtor's organizational status
□ Confirm no name change
□ Confirm secured party name unchanged
□ Run annual UCC-11 search
□ Review trust and LLC resolutions
□ Update administrative binder
□ Check continuation deadlines
□ Ensure collateral schedules reflect reality
□ Confirm no unauthorized filings appear

WORKBOOK

This workbook is designed to turn the information in the main guidebook into **practical skill**. Each module helps you:

- Think like a secured party
- Understand legal logic
- Draft accurate commercial language
- Avoid common mistakes
- Apply UCC rules to real scenarios
- Build enforcement-ready documentation

Use it as:

- A training tool
- A course companion
- A certification workbook
- A trust administration manual
- A personal study and application tool

Let's begin.

● MODULE 1 — Understanding the UCC Filing System

1. Analysis Questions

1. In your own words, what is the purpose of the UCC?

---

2. Why does the UCC rely on public notice instead of private evidence?

---

2. Scenario Exercise

A lender wants to make sure everyone knows it has a claim on a customer's equipment.
? What document must they file?

---

3. Drafting Task

Explain "public notice" in plain English:

---

4. Diagram Interpretation

WORKBOOK

Interpret the "Attachment → Perfection → Priority" diagram.

● MODULE 2 — What a UCC-1 Financing Statement Is

1. Analysis Questions

1. Why does a UCC-1 not create ownership?

2. What three core pieces of information must every UCC-1 contain?

2. Scenario Exercise

Debtor gives a lender rights in their inventory.
? What step perfects the lender's rights?

3. Drafting Task

Write a 1-sentence explanation of a UCC-1 for a beginner:

● MODULE 3 — When a UCC-1 Is Commonly Used

1. Analysis Questions

List three legitimate use cases:

1.
2.
3.

2. Scenario Exercise

A musician licenses their catalog and wants to secure royalty rights.
? Which collateral category applies?

3. Drafting Task

Draft a one-sentence filing purpose:

WORKBOOK

● MODULE 4 — Parties to a UCC-1 Filing

1. Analysis Questions

1. Why must the debtor name be exact?

---

2. Who can be a secured party?

---

2. Scenario Exercise

A trust is filing as secured party.
? Should the trustee's personal name be listed as debtor? Why or why not?

---

3. Drafting Task

Write a correct debtor line for a trust:

● MODULE 5 — Collateral Descriptions

1. Analysis Questions

1. What makes a collateral description "commercially acceptable"?

---

2. Scenario Exercise

Which is acceptable?

A: "All rights, sovereignty, and energy of the living man."
B: "All business equipment owned or later acquired."

Circle: A / B

3. Drafting Task

Draft a proper IP collateral description:

● MODULE 6 — Filing a UCC-1 Step-by-Step

1. Analysis Questions

What are the five steps of the filing process?

1. ____________________
2. ____________________
3. ____________________
4. ____________________
5. ____________________

2. Scenario Exercise

You filed a UCC-1 but forgot to save the receipt.
? What problem may occur later?

____

3. Drafting Task

Write a checklist for yourself before you click "Submit."

____

____

● MODULE 7 — Why Filings Become Ineffective

1. Analysis Questions

Which two errors destroy priority instantly?

1. ____________________
2. ____________________

2. Scenario Exercise

A debtor moved states; the secured party never re-filed.
? What happens after 4 months?

____

3. Drafting Task

Explain why precision matters:

____

____

● MODULE 8 — UCC-3 Amendments

1. Analysis Questions

List the four uses of a UCC-3:

1. ________________
2. ________________
3. ________________
4. ________________

2. Scenario Exercise

A company sells its interest in a loan portfolio.
? Which UCC-3 event happens?

---

3. Drafting Task

Write a sample "Assignment Amendment" note:

● MODULE 9 — Continuations, Corrections & Protective Filings

1. Analysis Questions

1. When must a continuation be filed?

---

2. Scenario Exercise

Your continuation was filed too early.
? What does the SOS do?

---

3. Drafting Task

Draft a correction purpose sentence:

● MODULE 10 — Assignments & Reorganization Filings

1. Analysis Questions

1. What is the advantage of an assignment vs. refiling?

---

2. Scenario Exercise

A holding trust takes over assets from an LLC.
? Which filing preserves priority?

---

3. Drafting Task

Write a "Full Assignment" statement:

● MODULE 11 — Terminations & Fraud Prevention

1. Analysis Questions

1. Who can authorize a termination?

---

2. Scenario Exercise

A debtor files an unauthorized termination.
? What is your first response?

---

3. Drafting Task

Write a protective filing notice:

● MODULE 12 — Liens, PMSIs & Purchase-Money Priority

1. Analysis Questions

What makes a PMSI special?

---

2. Scenario Exercise

A lender finances new equipment for a contractor.
? What type of interest applies?

---

3. Drafting Task

Write a PMSI collateral line:

WORKBOOK

● MODULE 13 — Securing Equipment, Vehicles & Movable Goods

1. Analysis Questions

How do vehicle title laws impact UCC filings?

---

2. Scenario Exercise

Company buys 10 forklifts. Lender files a UCC.
? Is the filing proper?

---

3. Drafting Task

Draft a collateral description for equipment inventory:

● MODULE 14 — Fixture Filings & Real Property Attachments

1. Analysis Questions

Where must fixture filings be recorded?

---

2. Scenario Exercise

Commercial ovens are bolted into a bakery floor.
? Fixture or not?

---

3. Drafting Task

Write a fixture filing location note:

● MODULE 15 — Accounts, Receivables & Intangibles

1. Analysis Questions

What is the difference between "account" and "payment intangible"?

---

2. Scenario Exercise

A consultant invoices clients monthly.
? What type of collateral is that?

---

3. Drafting Task

Write an acceptable collateral description for receivables:

● MODULE 16 — Trusts, Estates & Private Filers

1. Analysis Questions

Why must the *trust name* be debtor, not the trustee?

---

2. Scenario Exercise

A trust is administered in Illinois but owns property in Texas.
? Where is the UCC filed?

---

3. Drafting Task

Draft debtor listing for a trust + trustee:

● MODULE 17 — Intellectual Property & Digital Rights

1. Analysis Questions

Which IP rights can be secured under Article 9?

---

2. Scenario Exercise

A creator wants to secure their book royalties.
? What collateral class applies?

---

3. Drafting Task

Write a proper IP collateral description:

WORKBOOK

● MODULE 18 — Compliance, Recordkeeping & Rejection Avoidance

1. Analysis Questions

What is the #1 cause of filing rejection?

---

2. Scenario Exercise

A filing includes philosophical language.
? What happens?

---

3. Drafting Task

Write a clean, simple collateral description:

● MODULE 19 — Multi-State Filings & Debtor Location Rules

1. Analysis Questions

Why does collateral location usually not matter?

---

2. Scenario Exercise

A Nevada LLC operates in 10 states.
? Where must the UCC be filed?

---

3. Drafting Task

Draft a jurisdiction decision note:

● MODULE 20 — Enforcement & Litigation Strategy

1. Analysis Questions

Name three enforcement tools a secured party has:

1. ______________________________
2. ______________________________

WORKBOOK

3. ____________________

2. Scenario Exercise

Debtor defaults; secured party has a perfected filing.

? What is the first step?

____

3. Drafting Task

Draft a sample default notice:

____

ABOUT THE AUTHOR

Rodney Cortez Carroll™ is a trust architect, legal researcher, and historical truth-seeker committed to restoring the erased identity of Indigenous American descendants. With over two decades of independent research into administrative law, estate recovery, and cultural reclassification, he brings to *Paper Genocide* both lived experience and scholarly depth.

Through his work, Carroll exposes the bureaucratic machinery that systematically redefined Indigenous peoples as "Negro," "Colored," or "Black"—not by ancestry, but by administrative decree. He has studied the entanglement between legal codes, federal policy, and identity manipulation, and he provides pathways for remedy through trusts, affidavits, and lawful status correction.

He is also the founder and trustee of the **Rodney Cortez Carroll El Ali Living Trust**, through which he executes much of his advocacy, authorship, and administrative redress. His work empowers individuals to reclaim their inherited rights, titles, and cultural standing with clarity and lawful authority.

Paper Genocide is not just a book—it's a record, a roadmap, and a reclamation.

Contact Information:
rodney@marmionway.net
rodney@babylonindustries.net
779-902-2928

ABOUT THE AUTHOR

Websites

www.marmionway.org

www.babylonindustries.net

Social

TikTok = @aliel5220

Other works by Rodney Carroll™ can be found by clicking the links or on Amazon.com

- DOMESTIC WARFARE - THE WAR AGAINST SELF DETERMINATION
- PAPER GENOCIDE – THE LEGAL ERASURE OF INDIGENOUS PEOPLE
- HERMETICA UNVEILED – THE MASTER KEY TO THE EMERALD TABLETS
- REPLENISHING THE STREAM – OVERCOMING ERECTILE DYSFUNCTION NATURALLY
- FEATHERS & FEZZES THE RETURN OF THE OLD ONE'S THE ARCHITECT KINGS
- BORN OF BLOOD BOUND BY PAPER
- How To Lawfully Protect, Control & Monetize a Personal Name Using State Based IP& Commercial Law.

Made in the USA
Monee, IL
05 November 2026

67807087R00118